Discover
Bruges

The highlights of Bruges
The 10 classic places
that no one should miss!

Rozenhoedkaai, a living picture postcard

The Rozenhoedkaai links the Belfry to the city's network of canals ('reien'). So perhaps it was inevitable that the quay should become one of the most photogenic locations in all of Bruges. In fact, this spot is so special that it is almost impossible not to take a photograph: a living postcard that you can be a part of!

A quiet moment in the Beguinage

Some places are just too pretty for words. The Beguinage is one such a place. It really leaves you speechless. All you can do is wander around and admire its beauty. This walled oasis of religious calm, with its impressive courtyard garden, its wind-bent trees, its white painted gables and its limitless silence, will charm even the greatest cynic. All year round. *(Also see page 76-77.)*

Burg and City Hall: medieval opulence 09 43

The Burg is one of the city's most beautiful squares. For more than six centuries, Bruges has been governed from its 14th-century City Hall, one of the oldest and most venerable in the Low Countries. All this time this remarkable historic building has dominated this majestic square. Nowhere else will you be able to experience the city's wealth and affluence so strongly. *(Also see page 92.)*

The Flemish primitives: timeless beauty 27 39

In the 15th century – Bruges' Golden Age – the fine arts reached their highest form of expression. Famous names such as Jan van Eyck and Hans Memling came to live and work in the city. Today, you can still admire the magnificent paintings of these world-famous Flemish primitives, standing face to face with masterpieces that were created more than 500 years ago in the very heart of Bruges. *(Also see pages 84-85 and 90.)*

Wandering through the old Hansa Quarter

From the 13th to the 15th century, Bruges was an important trading centre at the crossroads between the Hansa cities of Scandinavia, England and Germany

(known collectively in those days as the 'Easterners') and the most important commercial regions in France, Spain and Italy. The Spanish traders established themselves at Spaanse Loskaai (Spanish Unloading Quay), while the Easterners set up shops on the Oosterlingenplein (Easterners' Square). Places where you can still feel the atmosphere of days long gone by.

🚢 The Canals of Bruges: the city's arteries

Experience the city by following an age-old tradition. Cruising Bruges' canals – the remarkable city arteries – you will discover secret gardens, picturesque bridges and wonderfully beautiful views. Although it sounds incredible, Bruges' loveliest places ooze even more charm when you admire them travelling by boat.

The Church of Our Lady: the centuries-old skyline of Bruges 15 35

The Church of Our Lady (Onze-Lieve-Vrouwekerk) is most remarkable for its 115,5 metre-high brick tower, a tribute to the skill of the city's medieval crafts-men and the second highest tower of its kind in the world. Inside the church you can wonder at the beauty of the *Madonna and Child*, a marble masterpiece sculpted by Michelangelo and guaranteed to leave no visitor unmoved. *(Also see page 87.)*

🏛 Almshouses: charity frozen in stone

Almshouses formed tiny villages within the city's ramparts. That's how these me-dieval residential courts – which are still occupied – are best described. Centuries ago they were built out of mortar and charity. Today their picturesque gardens, white façades and glorious silence are the city's havens of peace par excellence. *(Also see page 38.)*

Concert Hall or Culture with a capital C ⑰

This imposing and intriguing culture temple is a beacon of light and provides 't Zand, the square on which it stands, with a unique dynamic all on its own. Inside there is no elaborate theatrical decoration, but a simple, almost minimalist, auditorium with a 'symphonic' arrangement of chairs. In short, the ideal circumstances in which to enjoy classical concerts, jazz, dance or theatre. *(Also see page 95.)*

🐴 Market Square – a must
⑩ ⑤ ㉙

If there is only one place you can visit in Bruges, this is it. The Market Square is the beating heart of the city. The colourful guild houses, the clatter of horses' hooves, the rattling of the carriages and the dominating presence of the Belfry all combine to create a setting of great beauty and charm, which is part medieval and part modern. And if you are feeling energetic, you can still climb the 366 steps of the 83-metre high belfry tower, which will reward you with a spectacular panorama over the city and its surrounding hinterland. The Market is also the home of Historium, a top attraction that takes you back to the golden days of Bruges in the Middle Ages. The balcony on the first or the second floor has a fine view of the square, with its statue of Jan Breydel and Pieter de Coninck, two of the city's most important historical figures. *(For more information about the Belfry see also page 77 and about Historium see page 85.)*

History in a nutshell

The Market Square in Bruges, 17th century
(painting by Jan-Baptist Meunincxhove)

Water played a crucial role in the birth and development of Bruges. It was at this place that a number of streams converged to form the River Reie, which then flowed northwards towards the coastal plain. Through a series of tidal creeks, the river eventually reached the sea. Little wonder, then, that even as far back as Roman times there was already considerable seafaring activity in this region. This has been proven by the discovery of the remains of two seagoing ships from this period, dating from the second half of the 3rd century or the first half of the 4th century. Even so, it would be another five centuries before the name 'Bruges' first began to appear – the word being a derivative of the old-German word 'brugj', which means 'mooring place'.

Its growing importance also resulted in it becoming the main fortified residence of the counts of Flanders, so that from the 11th century onwards the city was not only a prosperous trading metropolis, but also a seat of considerable political power.

Taking off

When the city's direct link with the sea was in danger of silting-up in the 12th century, Bruges went through a period of anxiety. Fortunately, the new waterway of the Zwin brought relief. As a result, Bruges was able to call itself the most important trade centre of North-west Europe in the following century. The world's first stock exchange began business. Its financial exchanges took place on a square in front of the premises that belonged to Van der Beurse, a Bruges merchant family. In spite of the typical medieval maladies, from epidemics to political unrest and social inequality, the citizens of Bruges prospered, and soon the city developed a magnet-like radiation. Around 1340, the inner city numbered no fewer than 35.000 inhabitants.

Golden Age

Success continually increased. In the 15th century – Bruges' Golden Age – things improved further when the Royal House of Burgundy took up residence in the city. New luxury goods were produced and sold in abundance, and famous painters such as Jan van Eyck and Hans Memling – the great Flemish primitives – found their creative niche here.

The fine arts flourished, and besides a substantial number of fine churches and unique merchant houses, a monumental town hall was also erected. Bruges' success seemed imperishable.

Decline

The death of the popular Mary of Burgundy in 1482 marked a sudden change of fortune. The relationship between the citizens of Bruges and their lord, the widower Maximilian, turned sour. The Burgundian court left the city, with the international traders following in its wake. Long centuries of wars and changes of political power took their toll. By the middle of the 19th century Bruges had become an impoverished city. Remarkably enough, a novel was partly responsible for giving a boost to the revival of the city.

Revival

With great care, Bruges took its first steps into tourism. In *Bruges la Morte* (1892), Georges Rodenbach aptly describes Bruges as a somewhat sleepy, yet extremely mysterious place. Soon Bruges' magnificent patrimony was rediscovered and her mysterious intimacy turned out to be her greatest asset. Building on this enthusiasm, the city was provided with a new seaport, which was called Zeebrugge. The pulling power of Bruges proved to be a great success and UNESCO added the medieval city centre to its World Heritage list. The rest is history.

From early settlement to international trade centre (...-1200)

851 Earliest record of the city

863 Baldwin I takes up residence at Burg

1127 Charles the Good, Count of Flanders, is murdered in the Church of Saint Donatian; first town rampart; first Bruges city charter

1134 Creation of the Zwin – evolving from the Sincfal marshes – that links Damme with the sea

Bruges' Golden Age (1369-1500)

1369 Margaret of Dampierre marries Philip the Bold, Duke of Burgundy. Beginning of the Burgundian period

1384 Margaret succeeds her father Louis of Male

1430 Marriage of Duke Philip the Good with Isabella of Portugal; establishment of the Order of the Golden Fleece

1436 Jan van Eyck paints the panel *Madonna with Canon Joris van der Paele*

1482 Mary of Burgundy dies as a result of a fall with her horse

1488 Maximilian of Austria is locked up in Craenenburg House on Markt for a few weeks

851   1200   1300   1500

Bruges as the economic capital of Northwest Europe (1200-1400)

1245 Foundation of the Beguinage

1280 Reconstruction in stone of the Belfry after the destruction of its wooden predecessor

1297 Second town rampart

1302 Bruges Matins and Battle of the Golden Spurs

1304 First Procession of the Holy Blood

1376-1420 Construction of the City Hall

The city gets her second wind (1500-1578)

1506 The cloth merchant Jan Mouscron acquires Michelangelo's *Madonna and Child*

1528 Lancelot Blondeel designs the mantelpiece of the Liberty of Bruges

1548 Birth of the scientist Simon Stevin

1562 Marcus Gerards engraves the first printed town map of Bruges

1578 Bruges joins the rebellion against the Spanish king

An impoverished town in a pauperised Flanders (1584-1885)

- **1584** Bruges becomes reconciled with the Spanish king
- **1604** The Zwin is closed off
- **1713-1795** Austrian period
- **1717** Foundation of the Academy of Fine Arts, which formed the basis for the collection of the Groeninge Museum.
- **1795-1814** French period
- **1799** Demolition of Saint Donatian's Cathedral and renovation of Burg
- **1815-1830** United Kingdom of the Netherlands
- **1830** Independence of Belgium; birth of the poet Guido Gezelle
- **1838** First railway station

The new city (1971-...)

- **1971** Amalgamation Law incorporates former suburbs
- **1985** King Baudouin opens new sea lock at Zeebrugge
- **2000** Historic city centre is given World Heritage status; Euro 2000 (European Football Championship)
- **2002** Cultural Capital of Europe
- **2008** *In Bruges* is released worldwide in cinemas
- **2009** The Procession of the Holy Blood is granted Intangible Cultural Heritage status by UNESCO
- **2013** Bruges is the setting for the Bollywood blockbuster *Peekay*

1600 **1700** **1800** **1900** **2000**

Provincial town with revived ambitions (1885-1970)

- **1887** Unveiling of the statue of Jan Breydel and Pieter de Coninck (Markt)
- **1892** Publication of *Bruges la Morte* by Georges Rodenbach
- **1896** Start of the construction of the seaport
- **1897** Dutch becomes the official language

- **1902** First important exhibition of the Flemish primitives
- **1914-1918** The Great War: Bruges is a German naval base
- **1940-1945** The historic city centre survives Second World War almost unscathed
- **1958** First Pageant of the Golden Tree

Practical information

Brugge City Card

Get to know the city in all its many facets and save money at the same time! With the **Brugge City Card** you can visit 27 museums and attractions in Bruges for free. The boat tours on the canals (departures are only guaranteed during the period 1/3 to 14/11) or the tour on a City Tour minibus (only possible during the period 1/1 to 29/2 and 15/11 to 28/2/2017) are also free. In addition, the Brugge City Card also guarantees a discount of at least 25% on a three-day pass for De Lijn (bus service), on numerous concerts, dance and theatre productions, on rental bikes, on underground parking and on various museums, attractions and other places of interest in the area around Bruges.

HOW DOES IT WORK?

You choose the validity period of your **Brugge City Card**: **48 hours** or **72 hours**. In the chapters *Know your way around Bruges* and *Discoveries outside of Bruges* you will find a detailed overview of all the guided tours, attractions, museums and places of interest in and around the city. If you see a 🔲, you will get in **for free** with your Brugge City Card; a 🔲 means that you will **receive at least a 25% discount** on the individual price. What's more, in the free monthly event calendar you can find a helpful list of all the events that you can visit at reduced costs using your Brugge City Card. When you use your Brugge City Card for the first time, it is automatically activated. Once the validity period has elapsed, the card automatically stops working. You can only visit each attraction once. Bear in mind that many of the city's museums are closed on Monday.

WHAT DOES IT COST?

(48h) € 47.00   (72h) € 53.00

HOW TO ORDER?

Just drop by the ℹ tourist offices on the Markt (Market Square - Historium), 't Zand (Zand Square - Concert Hall) or the Stationsplein (Station Square - station) or order your Brugge City Card online via www.bruggecitycard.be

Bicycle rental points

Bauhaus Bike Rental
LOCATION > Langestraat 145
PRICE > 3 hours: € 6.00; full day: € 10.00
(Brugge City Card: € 6.00)
OPEN > Daily, 8.00 a.m.-7.00 p.m.
(bikes must be returned by 7.00 p.m.;
during summer by 9.00 p.m.)
INFO > Tel. +32 (0)50 34 10 93,
www.bauhaus.be/services/bike-rental

B-Bike Concertgebouw
LOCATION > Concertgebouw, 't Zand
PRICE > 1 hour: € 5.00; 4 hours: € 10.00;
full day: € 15.00 (Brugge City Card: € 11.25)
OPEN > During the period 15/3 to 1/11: daily,
10.00 a.m.-7.00 p.m.
INFO > Tel. +32 (0)479 97 12 80,
info@b-bike.be

Bruges Bike Rental
LOCATION > Niklaas Desparsstraat 17
PRICE > 1 hour: € 4.00; 2 hours: € 7.00;
4 hours: € 10.00; full day: € 13.00; students
(on display of a valid student card): € 10.00.
Price tandem, 1 hour: € 10.00; 2 hours:
€ 15.00; 4 hours: € 20.00; full day: € 25.00;
students (on display of a valid student
card): € 22.00

OPEN > During the period 1/2 to 28/12:
daily: 10.00 a.m.-8.00 p.m.
INFO > Tel. +32 (0)50 61 61 08,
www.brugesbikerental.be

De Ketting
LOCATION > Gentpoortstraat 23
PRICE > Full day: € 6.00. Price electric
bike, full day: € 20.00/day
OPEN > During the period 1/4 to 15/10:
Sunday and Monday, 10.30 a.m.-6.30 p.m.
and Tuesday to Saturday, 10.00 a.m.-
6.30 p.m.; during the period 16/10 to 31/3:
Monday, 10.30 a.m.-6.30 p.m. and Tuesday
to Saturday, 10.00 a.m.-6.30 p.m.
INFO > Tel. +32 (0)50 34 41 96,
www.deketting.be

Electric Scooters
Hire of electric bikes.
LOCATION > Gentpoortstraat 55 en 62
PRICE > 2 hours: € 10.00; 4 hours: € 18.00;
full day: € 30.00
OPEN > During the period 1/4 to 31/10:
Wednesday to Saturday, 10.00 a.m.-
6.00 p.m.
EXTRA > Rental of electric scooters
(see page 21)
INFO > Tel. +32 (0)474 09 19 18,
www.electric-scooters.be

Eric Popelier
LOCATION > Mariastraat 26
PRICE > 1 hour: € 5.00; 4 hours: € 10.00; full
day: € 15.00 (Brugge City Card: € 11.25).
Price electric bike or tandem, 1 hour: € 10.00;
4 hours: € 20.00; full day: € 30.00. Price reduction for students
OPEN > During the period 1/4 to 15/10:
daily, 9.00 a.m.-7.00 p.m.; during the
period 16/10 to 31/3: daily, 9.00 a.m.-
6.00 p.m.
ADDITIONAL CLOSING DATES > Closed on
Monday in January and December
INFO > Tel. +32 (0)50 34 32 62,
www.fietsenpopelier.be

🚲 Fietspunt Station
LOCATION > Hendrik Brugmansstraat 3
(Stationsplein, Railway station Square)
PRICE > 1 hour: € 6.00; 4 hours: € 10.00;
full day: € 15.00 (Brugge City Card: € 11.00).
Electric bike, 4 hours: € 20.00; full day:
€ 30.00
OPEN > Monday to Friday, 7.00 a.m-
7.30 p.m.; during the period 1/4 to 30/9:
also during weekends and on holidays,
10.00 a.m.-9.00 p.m.
ADDITIONAL CLOSING DATES >
1/1 to 3/1 and 24/12 to 31/12
INFO > Tel. +32 (0)50 39 68 26,
fietspunt.brugge@groepintro.be

🚲 Koffieboontje
LOCATION > Hallestraat 4
PRICE > 1 hour: € 5.00; 4 hours: € 10.00;
full day: € 15.00 (Brugge City Card: € 11.25);
students (on display of a valid student
card): € 11.25. Price tandem, 1 hour:
€ 10.00; 4 hours: € 20.00; full day: € 30.00;
students (on display of a valid student
card): € 22.50
OPEN > Daily, 9.00 a.m.-10.00 p.m.
INFO > Tel. +32 (0)50 33 80 27,
www.bikerentalkoffieboontje.be

🚲 Snuffel Hostel
LOCATION > Ezelstraat 42
PRICE > Full day: € 8.00 (Brugge City Card:
€ 6.00)
OPEN > Daily, 8.00 a.m.-8.00 p.m. (bikes
have to be returned by 8.00 p.m.)
INFO > Tel. +32 (0)50 33 31 33,
www.snuffel.be

Most of the bicycle rental points ask for the
payment of a guarantee.

Campers

The Kanaaleiland ('Canal Island') at the
Bargeweg offers excellent solid ground for
59 campers all year round. Once your camp-
er is parked, you are just a five-minute walk

from the city centre (via the Beguinage). The
parking area is open for new arrivals until
10.00 p.m. It is not possible to make prior
reservations.
PRICE > During the period 1/4 to 30/9:
€ 25.00/day; during the period 1/10 to 31/3:
€ 19.00/day. Free electricity; it is also possible to stock up with clean water (€ 0.50) and
dispose of dirty water.

Church services

**01 Basiliek van het Heilig Bloed
(Basilica of the Holy Blood)**
Daily (except Thursday): 11.00 a.m.

02 Begijnhofkerk (Beguinage Church)
Monday to Saturday: 7.15 a.m.,
Sunday: 9.30 a.m.

04 English Convent
Wednesday and Friday: 7.45 a.m.

12 English Church
('t Keerske / Saint Peter's Chapel)
English language Anglican service,
Sunday: 6.00 p.m.

08 Jeruzalemkapel (Jerusalem Chapel)
Saturday: 9.00 a.m.

09 Jezuïetenhuis (Jesuit House)
Monday to Friday: 12.00 p.m.,
Saturday: 5.00 p.m., Sunday: 11.30 a.m.

10 Kapucijnenkerk (Capuchins Church)
Monday to Friday: 8.00 a.m.
(Tuesday: also 6.00 p.m.), Saturday:
6.00 p.m., Sunday: 10.00 a.m.

**09 Kapel Hof Bladelin
(Chapel Bladelin Court)**
Monday to Friday: 8.00 a.m.

11 Karmelietenkerk
(Carmelites Church)
Monday to Friday 7.00 a.m. and 6.00 p.m.,
Saturday: 6.00 p.m., Sunday: 10.00 a.m.

15 Onze-Lieve-Vrouwekerk
(Church of Our Lady)
Saturday: 5.30 p.m., Sunday: 11.00 a.m.

16 Onze-Lieve-Vrouw-ter-Potteriekerk
(Church of Our Lady of the Pottery)
Sunday: 7.00 a.m. and 9.30 a.m.

17 Onze-Lieve-Vrouw-
van-Blindekenskapel
(Chapel of Our Lady of the Blind)
First Saturday of the month: 6.00 p.m.

18 Orthodoxe Kerk HH. Konstantijn
& Helena (Orthodox Church Saints
Constantin & Helen)
Saturday: 6.00 p.m., Sunday: 9.00 a.m.

19 Sint-Annakerk (Saint Anne's Church)
Sunday: 10.00 a.m.

20 Sint-Gilliskerk (Saint Giles' Church)
Sunday: 7.00 p.m.

22 Sint-Jakobskerk
(Saint Jacob's Church)
Wednesday and Saturday: 7.00 p.m.

23 Sint-Salvatorskathedraal
(Saint Saviour's Cathedral)
Monday to Friday: 6.00 p.m.
(Wednesday: also 9.00 a.m.),
Saturday: 4.00 p.m., Sunday: 10.30 a.m.

12 Verenigde Protestantse Kerk
(United Protestant Church)
('t Keerske / Saint Peter's Chapel)
Sunday: 10.00 a.m.

25 Vrije Evangelische Kerk
(Free Evangelical Church)
Sunday: 10.00 a.m.

Cinemas
» All films are shown in their original
language.

 Cinema Liberty
Kuipersstraat 23, www.cinema-liberty.be

 Cinema Lumière
Sint-Jakobsstraat 36, www.lumierecinema.be

11 Kinepolis Brugge
Koning Albert I-laan 200, Sint-Michiels,
www.kinepolis.com | scheduled bus: no. 27,
bus stop: Kinepolis

Climate
Bruges enjoys a mild, maritime climate. The
summers are warm without being hot and
the winters are cold without being freezing.
During spring and autumn the temperatures
are also pleasant and there is moderate
rainfall throughout the year, with the heavi-
est concentrations in autumn and winter. So
remember to bring your umbrella!

Emergencies
▶ **European emergency number**
» tel. 112. This general number is used in
all countries of the European Union to contact the emergency services: police, fire
brigade or medical assistance. The number operates 24 hours a day, 7 days a week.

▶ **Medical help**
» **Doctors, pharmacists, dentists and
nursing officers on duty**
tel. 1733
» **S.O.S. Emergency Service**
tel. 100
» **Hospitals**
A.Z. St.-Jan > tel. +32 (0)50 45 21 11
A.Z. St.-Lucas > tel. +32 (0)50 36 91 11
St.-Franciscus Xaveriuskliniek >
tel. +32 (0)50 47 04 70

» **Poisons Advice Centre**
tel. +32 (0)70 245 245

▶ **Police**
» **General telephone number**
tel. +32 (0)50 44 88 44
» **Emergency police assistance**   tel. 101
» **Working hours**
Monday to Friday: 8.00 a.m.-5.00 p.m.
and Saturday: 9.00 a.m.-6.00 p.m. you
can contact the central police services at
Kartuizerinnenstraat 4 | City map: E9
» **After working hours**
There is a 24/7 permanence at the police
station at the Lodewijk Coiseaukaai 3 |
City map: F1

Formalities

» **Identity**
An identity card or valid passport is necessary. Citizens of the European Union do not
require an entrance visa. If you arrive in
Belgium from outside the European Union,
you must first pass through customs.
There are no border controls once inside
the European Union.

» **Health**
Citizens of the European Union can use their
own national health insurance card/docu-
ment to obtain free medical treatment in
Belgium. You can obtain this card from your
own national health service. Please note,
however, that every member of the family
must have his/her own card/document.

Getting there
▶ **By car/coach/ferry**
From the UK you travel to Bruges by ferry
or by Eurotunnel:
» **Hull (UK) – Zeebrugge (B)** with P&O
Ferries (crossing: 12h00). Take the N31
from Zeebrugge to Bruges. Estimated
distance Zeebrugge – Bruges is 17 km or
11 miles (30 min driving).

» **Dover (UK) – Dunkerque (F)** with DFDS
Seaways (crossing: 2h00). Take the mo-
torway E40 to Bruges. Estimated distance Dunkerque – Bruges is 76 km or
47 miles (1h driving).
» **Dover (UK) – Calais (F)** with P&O Ferries or DFDS Seaways (crossing: 1h30).
Estimated distance Calais – Bruges is
120 km or 75 miles (1h30 driving).
» **Folkestone (UK) – Calais (F)** via Eurotunnel (35 min). Estimated distance
Calais – Bruges is 120 km or 75 miles
(1h30 driving).

**A 30 kph zone is in force throughout the
entire city centre. This means that you are
forbidden at all times to drive faster than
30 kilometres per hour.**
Parking is for an unlimited time and is most
advantageous in one of the two city centre car
parks. *(For more information, see 'Parking'.)*

▶ **By train**
» **National**
The station at Brussel-Zuid (Brussels South)
is the Belgian hub for international rail traf-
fic. Numerous high speed trains arrive in
Brussel-Zuid daily, coming from Paris
(Thalys and TGV), Lille (Eurostar and TGV),
London (Eurostar), Amsterdam (Thalys) and
Cologne (Thalys and ICE). Every hour two
trains for Ostend or Knokke/Blankenberge
(stopping at Bruges) depart from Brussel-
Zuid. The travelling time between Brussel-
Zuid and Bruges is approximately 1 hour.

▶ **By plane**
» **Via Brussels Airport**
Each day, the national airport at Zaventem
welcomes flights from more than 200 cities
in 66 countries. It is easy to travel from
Brussels national airport to Bruges by train.
On weekdays, there is a direct hourly ser-
vice. You can also take the Brussels Airport
Express (four trains every hour) to Brussel-
Noord (Brussels-North), Brussel-Centraal
(Brussels-Central) or Brussel-Zuid (Brus-

▶ How to get to Bruges?

departure	via	km	mls	time train ☻	time bus ☻	time boat ☻	make a reservation
Amsterdam	Brussels-South/-Midi	253	157	03:11	-	-	www.b-europe.com
Brussels Airport	-	110	68	01:29	-	-	www.belgianrail.be
Brussels South Charleroi Airport	-	148	92	-	02:10	-	www.flibco.com
Ostend-Bruges Airport	Oostende	24	15	See page 17	See page 17	-	www.belgianrail.be, www.wheelexpress.be
Dover	Dunkerque	-	-	-	-	02:00	www.dfds.com
Dover	Calais	-	-	-	-	01:30	www.poferries.com, www.dfds.com
Hull	Zeebrugge	-	-	-	-	1 night	www.poferries.com
Lille Flandres	Kortrijk	75	47	01:47	-	-	www.b-europe.com
London St Pancras	Brussels-South/-Midi	-	-	03:30	-	-	www.eurostar.com

sels-South). Every hour, two trains leave from these stations for Ostend or Knokke/Blankenberge, stopping in Bruges. For more information on timetables and rates, please refer to www.b-rail.be. Provided you have reserved in advance, taxi rides to and from Brussels national airport are available from Bruges taxi services at a fixed rate of € 200.00 (price adjustments are possible throughout the year).

» **Via Brussels South Charleroi Airport**

This popular regional airport receives multiple low cost flights every day from various cities and regions in Europe. The Flibco.com bus company (www.flibco.com) provides a direct shuttle bus service to and from the station in Bruges, with a frequency of 9 trips per day (there and back). The shuttle bus is comfortable, fast and cheap. If you book in advance (online), it is even cheaper. The Bruges taxi services drive to and from Brussels South Charleroi Airport at a fixed rate of € 250.00 (price adjustments throughout the year are possible). Reservations must be made in advance.

» **Via Ostend-Bruges Airport**

Ostend-Bruges Airport is developing rapidly and is systematically developing its range of flights and services. The railway station at Ostend is just a 15-minute bus ride away. From here, there are at least three trains to Bruges each hour between 6.00 a.m. and 10.00 p.m., with final destinations in Eupen, Welkenraedt, Brussels national airport, Antwerp-Central or Kortrijk. The travelling time to Bruges is approx. 15 minutes. Please consult www.belgianrail.be for more information about timetables and fares.

For some flights with early/late departure/arrival times, there is a shuttle service that travels to and from Bruges. Tickets (single/return) can be purchased in the airport at offices of Wheel Express at the fixed rate of € 10.00 per person and per trip.

Taxi rides to and from Bruges with the Bruges and Ostend taxi services (advance reservation is required) are charged at the fixed rate of € 70.00. Prices may be adjusted in the course of the year.

» In Bruges

From the station in Bruges, you can travel to your overnight accommodation address by bus (every five minutes; *see the section 'Public transport'*) or by taxi (*see 'Taxis'*).

Good to know

With its wide shopping streets, inviting terraces, trendy eating houses and stylish hotels, Bruges is a paradise for shoppers. Don't let pickpockets ruin your shopping day. Always keep your **wallet/purse** in a closed inside pocket, and not in an open handbag or rucksack. A golden tip for ladies: always close your handbag and wear it with the fastener against your body. Bruges is a lively, fun-loving city, with great nightlife. There are plenty of places where you can amuse yourself until the early hours of the morning. Please bear in mind that it is prohibited to sell, give or serve **spirits** (whisky, gin, rum, vodka, etc.) to persons under the age of 18 years. For persons under the age of 16, this prohibition applies for all drinks with an alcohol content exceeding 0.5%. When purchasing alcohol, proof of age may be requested. All drugs – including cannabis – are prohibited by law in Belgium. Visiting Bruges means endless hours of fun, but please allow the visitors who come after you to enjoy their fun in a **clean** and **tidy** city: so always put your rubbish in a rubbish bin.

🛈 Info on the go

In Bruges, 99 taxi drivers, coachmen and boatmen can call themselves 'touristic ambassadors of the city' following their successful completion of the course 'info on the go', which is all about customer-friendliness and an excellent knowledge of the city and its sights. These ambassadors can be identified by the 'info on the go' logo.

Inhabitants

On 1 January 2015, there were 19,418 inhabitants registered as living in the inner city of Bruges. The total population of Greater Bruges on the same date was 117,797.

🔒 Lockers

» Station (railway station)

Stationsplein | City map: C13

» 29 Historium

Markt 1

Market days

» Monday

8.00 a.m.-1.30 p.m. | Onder de Toren-Lissewege | miscellaneous

» Wednesday

8.00 a.m.-1.30 p.m. | Markt | food and flowers

» Friday

8.00 a.m.-1.30 p.m. | Market Square - Zeebrugge | miscellaneous

» Saturday

8.00 a.m.-1.30 p.m. | 't Zand and Beursplein | miscellaneous

» Sunday

7.00 a.m.-2.00 p.m. | Veemarkt, Sint-Michiels | miscellaneous

» Tuesday to Saturday

8.00 a.m.-1.30 p.m. | Vismarkt | fish

» Daily

8.00 a.m.-7.00 p.m. | Vismarkt | artisanal products

» **Saturday, Sunday, public holidays and bridge days in the period 15/3 to 15/11 + also on Friday in the period June to September**
10.00 a.m.-6.00 p.m. | Dijver | antique, bric-à-brac and crafts

Money

Most of the banks in Bruges are open from 9.00 a.m. to 12.30 p.m. and from 2.00 p.m. to 4.30 p.m. Many branch offices are also open on Saturday morning, but on Sunday they are all closed. There are cash points in several shopping streets, on 't Zand, Simon Stevinplein, Stationsplein (Railway station Square) and on Bargeplein. You can easily withdraw money from cash machines with Visa, Eurocard or MasterCard. Currency can be exchanged in every bank or in an exchange office. In the event of the loss or theft of your bank or credit card, it is best to immediately block the card by calling Card Stop on tel. 070 344 344 (24 hours a day).
» **Exchange office Goffin Change**
Steenstraat 2 | City map: E8
» **Exchange office Pillen bvba**
Vlamingstraat 18 | City map: E7
» **Exchange office Rozenhoedkaai**
Rozenhoedkaai 2 | City map: F8

Opening hours

Most shops open their doors at 10.00 a.m. and close at 6.00 p.m. or 6.30 p.m. from Monday to Saturday. Some shops are also open on Sunday afternoon. Nowadays, there are even more shops open during shopping Sundays *(see page 27)*.
Cafés and restaurants have no (fixed) closing hour. Sometimes they will remain open until the early hours of the morning and other days they will close earlier: it all depends on the number of customers.

Parking

Bruges is a city on a human scale. The use of motor vehicles in the historic inner city is not recommended and street parking above ground is limited in time to a maximum of 4 hours in the Blue Zone and to 2 hours in the Pay&Display Zones. You can easily park your car in one of the underground car parks, which is usually less expensive. Parking for an unlimited time is cheapest in one of the two city centre car parks: at the front side (City map: D13) of the station (€ 3.50/ 24 hours) or under 't Zand (€ 8.70/24 hours). Both are situated within walking distance of the city centre, but you can also use the bus transfer with De Lijn *(read more under the section 'Public transport')* between the parking Centrum-Station and the city centre (included in your parking fee for 4 passengers). The Park and Ride areas are situated right outside of the city centre. Here you can park your car for free and for a longer duration. The city centre is a stone's throw away on foot or by bus. If you are staying in Bruges, ask about parking spots near your place of accommodation in advance. Holders of a Brugge City Card (www.bruggecitycard.be) receive a 25% discount at the underground car parks Centrum-Station, Centrum-'t Zand, Katelijne and Pandreitje operated by Interparking.

▶ Parking Centrum-Station
Stationsplein | City map: D13
CAPACITY > 1500
OPEN > Daily, 24 hours a day
PRICE > Maximum € 3.50/24 hrs (Brugge City Card: a discount of 25 %) | hourly rate: € 0.70 | including free bus transfer (max. 4 persons per car)

▶ Parking Centrum- t Zand
under 't Zand | City map: C9
CAPACITY > 1400
OPEN > Daily, 24 hours a day
PRICE > Maximum € 8.70/24 hrs (Brugge City Card: a discount of 25 %) | hourly

rate: € 1.20; from the second hour you pay per quarter. Check www.interparking.com for any updates.

Post offices

» **bpost Markt**
Markt 5 | City map: E8
» **bpost Beursplein**
Sint-Maartensbilk 14 | City map: B10
In the course of 2016, both offices will move to their new location at Smedenstraat 57 | City map: B9
For posting letters, cards, etc. and for the purchase of stamps you can go to one of the postal points or stamp shops that you will find in various shopping streets throughout the city.

Public holidays

Belgium has quite a lot of public holidays. On these holidays most companies, shops, offices and public services are closed.
» 1 January (New Year's Day)
» 27 March (Easter Sunday) and 28 March (Easter Monday)
» 1 May (Labour Day)
» 5 May (Ascension Day)
» 15 May (Whit Sunday) and 16 May (Whit Monday)
» 11 July (Flemish regional holiday)
» 21 July (Belgian national holiday)
» 15 August (Assumption of Mary)
» 1 November (All Saints' Day)
» 11 November (Armistice Day)
» 25 December (Christmas)
» 26 December (Boxing Day)

Public transport

▶ 🚌 **Bus**
You can use public transport during your stay. De Lijn connects the railway station and the centre by bus every five minutes. From the Bargeplein (City map: E13), close to the spot where the tourist buses stop, there are also frequent services to the station and the

city centre. The most important of the city's bus stops are marked with a bus pictogram on the foldout map at the back of this guide. **Please note**: on Saturdays and every first Sunday of the month (10.00 a.m.-6.00 p.m.), there are no buses on the central axis Zuidzandstraat, Steenstraat, Geldmuntstraat and Noordzandstraat. A ticket allows you to change bus services as many times as you want for a period of 60 minutes. The ticket price is € 3.00. With the Brugge City Card (www.bruggecitycard.be), you can purchase a three-day pass for all De Lijn services for € 8.00. This pass is valid on all buses and trams in Flanders. You can buy the pass – like the Brugge City Card – from the
🛈 tourist offices on the Markt, 't Zand and the Stationsplein. All De Lijn tickets (except the three day pass purchased at the special rate with the Brugge City Card) can be bought at the following points of sale.

▶ Tickets
» **Advance sales offices**
De Lijnwinkel, Stationsplein
🛈 Tourist office on 't Zand (Concertgebouw)
Various book stores, newsagents and supermarkets in the city centre
» **Vending machines De Lijn**
De Lijnwinkel, Stationsplein
Bus stop, 't Zand
» **Info** www.delijn.be

Scooter rental

Electric Scooters

Rental of electric scooters (max. speed: 25 kph).

LOCATION > Gentpoortstraat 55 and 62
PRICE > 2 hours: € 35.00; 4 hours: € 50.00; full day: € 65.00 (Brugge City Card: € 48.75)
OPEN > During the period 1/4 to 31/10: Wednesday to Saturday, 10.00 a.m.-6.00 p.m.
CONDITIONS > Minimum driver age = 23 years
EXTRA > Rental of electric bikes (see page 13)
INFO > Tel. +32 (0)474 09 19 18, www.electric-scooters.be

Vespatours

LOCATION > Concertgebouw, 't Zand
PRICE > Including helmet and insurance, half day: € 50.00 (1 person per Vespa) or € 70.00 (2 persons per Vespa); full day: € 70.00 (1 person per Vespa) or € 80.00 (2 persons per Vespa)
OPEN > During the period 1/3 to 15/11: daily, 10.00 a.m.-6.00 p.m.
CONDITIONS > Minimum driver age = 21 years, driver's license B
EXTRA > Guided tours (see page 157)
INFO > Tel. +32 (0)497 64 86 48, www.vespatours-brugge.be

Scooter rental points usually demand a deposit before departure.

Smoking

In Belgium there is a general ban on smoking in cafés, restaurants, the public areas in hotels (lobby, bar, corridors, etc.) and in all public buildings (train stations, airports, etc.). Those unable to kick the habit will usually find an ashtray just outside (often under shelter).

ℹ️ Tourist offices

There are three tourist information offices in Bruges: one in the Historium (Market Square), one in the Concertgebouw (Concert Hall) and a third in the railway station.

» Tourist office Markt (Historium)
Markt 1
Daily, 10.00 a.m.-5.00 p.m.
» Tourist office 't Zand (Concertgebouw)
't Zand
Monday to Saturday, 10.00 a.m.-5.00 p.m.
Sunday and public holidays, 10.00 a.m.-2.00 p.m.
» Tourist office Stationsplein (Station)
Stationsplein
Daily, 10.00 a.m.-5.00 p.m.

All tourist offices are closed on Christmas Day and New Year's Day. For more information: tel. +32 (0)50 44 46 46, toerisme@brugge.be, www.visitbruges.be

Swimming pools

11 Interbad

Six 25-meter lanes; also a recreational pool, water slide, toddler's pool and teaching pool.
INFO > Veltemweg 35, Sint-Kruis, tel. +32 (0)50 35 07 77, interbad@skynet.be, www.interbad.be; scheduled bus no. 10, no. 58 or no. 58S, bus stop: Watertoren

12 Jan Guilini

25-meter indoor pool in a beautiful listed building, named after the swimming champion and resistance fighter Jan Guilini.
INFO > Keizer Karelstraat 41, tel. +32 (0)50 31 35 54, zwembadjanguilini@brugge.be, www.brugge.be/sport; scheduled bus no. 9, bus stop: Visartpark

13 S&R Olympia

In addition to a 50-meter sports pool, S&R Olympia offers extensive recreational facilities in the 'sub-tropical swimming paradise'. In fine weather, you can use the large lawn with its two outdoor pools and various other attractions.

INFO > Doornstraat 110, Sint-Andries, tel. +32 (0)50 67 28 70, olympia@sr-olympia.be, www.sr-olympia.be; scheduled bus no. 25, bus stop: Jan Breydel or no. 5, bus stop: Lange Molen

All information about opening times is available at the  tourist office Markt (Historium), 't Zand (Concertgebouw) or Stationsplein (Station, railway station).

Taxis

Whoever takes a taxi in Bruges with the logo 'info on the go' can enjoy all the benefits of a Certified Info Driver. As 'ambassadors' for Bruges, these taxidrivers will tell you with great enthusiasm all about their city and will help to put you in just the right mood for your city visit.

🚕 **TAXI STANDS**
» At Bruges station: city centre side and Sint-Michiels side
» At the Bargeweg (Kanaaleiland)
» On the Markt
» In the Adriaan Willaertstraat

PRICE > The local taxi companies all use the same fixed rate tariffs (adjustments are possible throughout the year):

Bruges <> Brussels Airport: € 200.00
Bruges <> Brussels South Charleroi
    Airport: € 250.00
Bruges <> Aéroport de Lille: € 140.00
Bruges <> Ostend-Bruges Airport:
    € 70.00

Please note: when you want to take a taxi from one of the airports to Bruges, you can only benefit from the above tariffs if you book the taxi in advance.

Telephoning

If you want to phone someone in Bruges from abroad, you must first dial the country code (00)32, followed by the zone code 50, and the number of the person you want. To phone Bruges from inside Belgium, you dial 050 plus the number of the person.

Toilets

There are a number of public toilets in Bruges (see the fold-out plan at the back of the guide). Some are accessible for wheelchair users. You will also find (free) toilets in some of the larger department stores or at the station. When local people need the toilet, they often pop into a cafe or pub to order something small so that they can use the facilities there.

Travelling season

Although most visitors come to the city in the spring and summer months, Bruges has something to offer all year round. The misty months of autumn and winter are ideal for atmospheric strolls along the canals and the cobbled streets, before ending up in a cosy restaurant or cheerful pub. The 'cold' months are also perfect for undisturbed visits to the city's many museums and sites of interest, before again finishing up in one of those same restaurants or pubs! What's more, in January, February and March you can get great discounts on many accommodation outlets in Bruges.

Bruges for bon-vivants

Bruges is a paradise for food connoisseurs. Its culinary delights range from Michelin-star establishments of international quality and reputation, through stylish local bistros and brasseries, to traditional Italian or Asian specialty restaurants.

Award winning restaurants

Bruges is one of the gastronomic centres of Europe and boasts an impressive number of star-rated restaurants. Whether you swear by fish or prefer meat; whether you love beer in your dishes or would rather have a wine-based sauce; whether you are a fan of exotic culinary delights or a devotee of authentic, local cooking, the superior kitchens in Bruges have so much to offer that everyone will be able to discover recipe to his or her taste.

» **De Karmeliet**   Langestraat 19, 8000 Brugge, tel. +32 (0)50 33 82 59,
   www.dekarmeliet.be (3 Michelin-stars, 17/20 graded by GaultMillau),
   closes in autumn 2016
» **De Jonkman**   Maalse Steenweg 438, 8310 Sint-Kruis, tel. +32 (0)50 36 07 67,
   www.dejonkman.be (2 Michelin-stars, 18/20 graded by GaultMillau)
» **Den Gouden Harynck**   Groeninge 25, 8000 Brugge, tel. +32 (0)50 33 76 37,
   www.goudenharynck.be (1 Michelin-star, 17/20 graded by GaultMillau)

» **Sans Cravate**   Langestraat 159, 8000 Brugge, tel. +32 (0)50 67 83 10, www.sanscravate.be (1 Michelin-star, 16/20 graded by GaultMillau)

» **Auberge De Herborist**   De Watermolen 15, 8200 Sint-Andries, tel. +32 (0)50 38 76 00, www.aubergedeherborist.be (1 Michelin-star, 15/20 graded by GaultMillau)

» **A'Qi**   Gistelse Steenweg 686, 8200 Sint-Andries, tel. +32 (0)50 30 05 99, www.restaurantaqi.be (1 Michelin-star, 15/20 graded by GaultMillau)

» **Zeno**   Vlamingstraat 53, 8000 Brugge, tel. +32 (0)50 68 09 93, www.restaurantzeno.be (16/20 graded by GaultMillau)

» **Goffin**   Maalse Steenweg 2, 8310 Sint-Kruis, tel. +32 (0)50 68 77 88, www.timothygoffin.be (15/20 graded by GaultMillau)

» **L.E.S.S.**   Torhoutse Steenweg 479, 8200 Sint-Michiels, tel. +32 (0)50 69 93 69, www.l-e-s-s.be (15/20 graded by GaultMillau)

» **Patrick Devos**   Zilverstraat 41, 8000 Brugge, tel. +32 (0)50 33 55 66, www.patrickdevos.be (15/20 graded by GaultMillau)

» **Bistro Bruut**   Meestraat 9, 8000 Brugge, tel. +32 (0)50 69 55 09, www.bistrobruut.be (14/20 graded by GaultMillau)

» **Bistro Refter**   Molenmeers 2, 8000 Brugge, tel. +32 (0)50 44 49 00, www.bistrorefter.be (14/20 graded by GaultMillau and selected as a Bib Gourmand)

» **bonte B**   Dweersstraat 12, 8000 Brugge, tel. +32 (0)50 34 83 43, www.restaurantbonteb.be (14/20 graded by GaultMillau)

» **Floris**   Gistelse Steenweg 520, 8200 Sint-Andries, tel. +32 (0)50 73 60 20, www.florisrestaurant.be (14/20 graded by GaultMillau)

» **La Tâche**   Blankenbergse Steenweg 1, 8000 Sint-Pieters, tel. +32 (0)50 68 02 52, www.latache.be (14/20 graded by GaultMillau)

» **'t Pandreitje**   Pandreitje 6, 8000 Brugge, tel. +32 (0)50 33 11 90, www.pandreitje.be (14/20 graded by GaultMillau)

» **Rock Fort**   Langestraat 15, 8000 Brugge, tel. +32 (0)50 33 41 13, www.rock-fort.be (14/20 graded by GaultMillau)

» **Tanuki**   Oude Gentweg 1, 8000 Brugge, tel. +32 (0)50 34 75 12, www.tanuki.be (14/20 graded by GaultMillau)

» **Tête Pressée**   Koningin Astridlaan 100, 8200 Sint-Michiels, tel. +32 (0)470 21 26 27, www.tetepressee.be (14/20 graded by GaultMillau and selected as a Bib Gourmand)

» **Assiette Blanche**   Philipstockstraat 23-25, 8000 Brugge, tel. +32 (0)50 34 00 94, www.assietteblanche.be (13/20 graded by GaultMillau and selected as a Bib Gourmand)

- » **Bhavani**   Simon Stevinplein 5, 8000 Brugge, tel. +32 (0)50 33 90 25, www.bhavani.be (13/20 graded by GaultMillau)
- » **De Mangerie**   Oude Burg 20, 8000 Brugge, tel. +32 (0)50 33 93 36, www.mangerie.com (13/20 graded by GaultMillau)
- » **De Visscherie**   Vismarkt 8, 8000 Brugge, tel. +32 (0)50 33 02 12, www.visscherie.be (13/20 graded by GaultMillau)
- » **Le Mystique**   Niklaas Desparsstraat 11, 8000 Brugge, tel. +32 (0)50 44 44 45, www.lemystique.be (13/20 graded by GaultMillau)
- » **Lieven**   Philipstockstraat 45, 8000 Brugge, tel. +32 (0)50 68 09 75, www.etenbijlieven.be (13/20 graded by GaultMillau)
- » **'t Zwaantje**   Gentpoortvest 70, 8000 Brugge, tel. +32 (0)473 71 25 80, www.hetzwaantje.be (13/20 graded by GaultMillau)
- » **De Florentijnen**   Academiestraat 1, 8000 Brugge, tel. +32 (0)50 67 75 33, www.deflorentijnen.be (recommended by GaultMillau)
- » **Duc de Bourgogne**   Huidenvettersplein 12, 8000 Brugge, tel. +32 (0)50 33 20 38, www.ducdebourgogne.be (recommended by GaultMillau)
- » **Huyze Die Maene**   Markt 17, 8000 Brugge, tel. +32 (0)50 33 39 59, www.huyzediemaene.be (recommended by GaultMillau)
- » **'t Jong Gerecht**   Langestraat 119, 8000 Brugge, tel. +32 (0)50 31 32 32, www.tjonggerecht.be (recommended by GaultMillau)
- » **Kwizien Divien**   Hallestraat 4, 8000 Brugge, tel. +32 (0)50 34 71 29, www.kwiziendivien.be (recommended by GaultMillau)
- » **Parkrestaurant**   Minderbroedersstraat 1, 8000 Brugge, tel. +32 (0)497 80 18 72, www.parkrestaurant.be (recommended by GaultMillau)
- » **'t Apertje**   Damse Vaart Zuid 223, 8310 Sint-Kruis, tel. +32 (0)50 35 00 12, www.apertje.be (selected as a Bib Gourmand)
- » **Kok au Vin**   Ezelstraat 21, 8000 Brugge, tel. +32 (0)50 33 95 21, www.kok-au-vin.be (selected as a Bib Gourmand)
- » **Kurt's Pan**   Sint-Jakobsstraat 58, 8000 Brugge, tel. +32 (0)50 34 12 24, www.kurtspan.be (selected as a Bib Gourmand)
- » **Pergola**   Meestraat 7, 8000 Brugge, tel. +32 (0)50 44 76 50, www.restaurantpergola.be (selected as a Bib Gourmand)

More tips on finding the right address for you can be found in the section 'Tips from Bruges connoisseurs'. Pages 108-109, 116-117, 124-125, 132-133, 140-141

Shopping in Bruges

Bruges has lots of shops to offer you something special: authentic places that surprise you again and again with their clever and original products. The city guarantees a harmonious mix of creative boutiques, trendy newcomers and classic names that have been professionally managed by the same family for generations.

Where to shop?

Because Bruges is pedestrian-friendly and the main streets are all close to each other, a day's shopping here is much more relaxing than in many other cities. You will find all the major national and international chains, as well as trendy local boutiques. And if you leave the beaten shopping paths you will certainly make plenty of interesting new discoveries. The most important shopping streets (indicated in yellow on the removable city map) run between the Market Square and the old city gates: Steenstraat, Simon Stevinplein, Mariastraat, Zuidzandstraat, Sint-Jakobsstraat, Sint-Amandsstraat, Geldmuntstraat, Noordzandstraat, Smedenstraat, Vlamingstraat, Philipstockstraat, Academiestraat, Hoogstraat, Langestraat and Katelijnestraat. There is also a small but elegant shopping centre, the Zilverpand, hidden between Noordzandstraat and Zuidzandstraat. Each neighbourhood has its own unique atmosphere. In Steenstraat, for example, you will find the famous brand names, whereas Langestraat boasts many little second-hand and bric-à-brac shops. The large hypermarkets are located just outside the city centre.

Shopping Sundays

Even on Sunday, you don't need to leave Bruges empty-handed. Many Bruges shops are usually open on Sunday *(see page 19)*, but on Shopping Sundays (every first Sunday of the month, public holidays excepted, from 1.00 p.m. to 6.00 p.m.) there are even more!

Bruges 'makers' and specialty stores

Creativity is built into the DNA of the people of Bruges; so it should come as no surprise to anyone that nowadays the city is teeming with innovative entrepreneurs. In the charming craft shops you are guaranteed to find an original, handmade gift to surprise your family and friends back home. Surf to www.handmadeinbrugge.be and discover dozens of great addresses and inspiring stories. The brand new city app Xplore Bruges also takes you to the city's old and new creative 'breeding grounds'. And as if this were not enough, at www.visitbruges.be you

can find another 50 unforgettable shopping addresses in Bruges city centre: a mix of authentic shops offering products that are made in Bruges and renowned specialty stores that have already been focusing on a single product (line) for more than 25 years.

Off to the market

There is nothing quite as delightful as shopping at a local market. In Bruges, this is possible almost every day. On Wednesday there is a food market on the Market Square from 8.00 a.m. to 1.30 p.m. On Saturday (8.00 a.m.-1.30 p.m.) the Zand Square and the Beursplein are taken over by a large food and general market (flowers, animals, clothing, etc.). And on Sunday, from 7.00 a.m. to 2.00 p.m., you can visit the food and general market on the Veemarkt, near the Koningin Astridlaan in the Sint-Michiels district. Every

morning (8.00 a.m.-1.30 p.m.) from Tuesday to Saturday, you can buy fresh fish and fish dishes at the Vismarkt (Fish Market). Finally, during the weekends and on public holidays from mid-March to mid-November, you can browse at the second-hand and craft market along the Dijver (10.00 a.m.-6.00 p.m.). If you love old bric-à-brac and antiques, you should definitely visit the 'Zandfeesten', the largest second-hand and craft market in Belgium, which is organized three times each summer (in early July, early August and late September) on the Zand Square and in the Koning Albertpark *(also see page 18)*.

Typical Bruges souvenirs

Bruges was a flourishing centre of the diamond trade as early as the 14th century, and the city also boasted a number of professional diamond-cutting establishments. In the diamond laboratory of the Bruges Diamond Museum, you will learn how all that sparkling splendour is assessed and processed. You might even find some glittering ideas for a little investment of your own!

Brugsch Swaentje

After that, it's only a matter of checking out the museum shop or the many other jewellery stores in the city with a keen connoisseur's eye before making your move - and cashing in! *You can find more information about the Bruges Diamond Museum on page 82.*

Since time immemorial, lace has also been inextricably connected to Bruges. Once upon a time, as many as a quarter of all the women in the city were employed making lace. Nowadays, you can still see female lace-makers in action in several of the Bruges lace shops. *You can find more information about lace and the Lace Centre on page 86 and in the interview with Kumiko Nakazaki on pages 120-123.*

The people of Bruges love to drink an occasional glass of beer. As a result, Bruges can boast a number of its own city-made beers. *Straffe Hendrik* and *Brugse Zot* are brewed in the Halve Maan Brewery, right in the heart of the historic city centre, while *Fort Lapin 8* and *Fort Lapin 10* are brewed in the Fort Lapin Brewery on the outskirts of town. *You can find more information about the Halve Maan Brewery on page 79, the Bruges Beer Museum on page 79 and the Bruges Beer Festival on pages 96-97.*

Perhaps you are not such a fan of beer? Those with a sweet tooth can visit one of the more than 50 chocolate boutiques that cater to all tastes: from deliciously old-fashioned chocolate blocks, through finger-licking good pralines that melt in your mouth, to ingenious molecular chocolate preparations tailored to the requirements of the city's star chefs. *Read more about chocolate on page 80.*

Spinolarei and
Jan van Eyckplein

Walking in
Bruges

Walk 1
Bruges,
proud World Heritage City

Bruges may be, quite rightly, very proud of her World Heritage status, but the city is happily embracing the future too! This walk takes you along world-famous panoramic views, sky-high monuments and centuries-old squares invigorated by contemporary constructions. One foot planted in the Middle Ages, the other one firmly planted in the present. This walk is an absolute must for first-time visitors who would like to explore the very heart of the city straight away. Keep your camera at the ready!

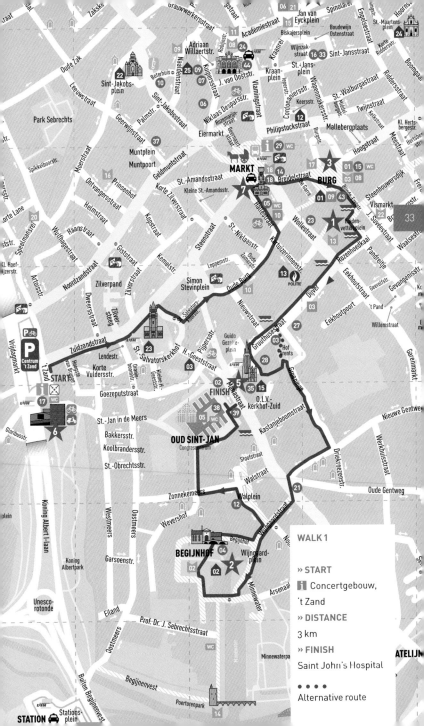

From 't Zand to Simon Stevinplein

This walk starts at the 🛈 tourist office 't Zand (Concertgebouw).

't Zand is dominated by the concert hall , one of Bruges' most talked-about buildings. Clear-cut proof that this World Heritage city isn't afraid of the future. On the very top floor of this modern cube-shaped building you can find the Concertgebouw – Open Huis (Concert Hall - Open House, from September 2016 onwards). Don't forget to drop in at 🛈 't Zand (Concertgebouw) on the ground floor: here you will find all the necessary tourist information as well as expert advice on all cultural events.

Leave 🛈 't Zand (Concertgebouw) behind you, walk along the square and turn into Zuidzandstraat, the first street on the right. Saint Saviour's Cathedral 23 looms up ahead on your right after three hundred metres.

TIP

From 2016 onwards, you should certainly pop in to the Concert Hall - Open House to take a look behind the scenes of this prestigious culture temple. In the Sound Factory, on the upper floor you can experiment with sounds and instruments.

Bruges' oldest parish church is located on a lower level than the present Zuidzandstraat, which is situated on an old sand ridge. What's more, in the Middle Ages people simply threw their refuse out onto the street where it was then flattened by passing carts and coaches. This raised the street level still further. Inside Saint Saviour's, the church tower's wooden rafters can be lit. The cathedral treasury displays and interesting copper memorial plaques, fine examples of gold and silver and paintings by Dieric Bouts, Hugo van der Goes and Pieter Pourbus.

Continue past the cathedral and walk down Sint-Salvatorskerkhof immediately on the right. Turn left into Sint-Salvatorskoorstraat. The Simon Stevinplein opens up at the end of this street.

This attractive square, lined with cosy restaurant terraces in summertime, is named after Simon Stevin, a wellknown Flemish-Dutch scientist. His gracious statue naturally takes centre stage.

Markt and Burg

Continue down Oude Burg, a street in the right-hand corner of the square. Before long you will see the Cloth Halls **10** on your left. These belong to the Belfry **05**. You're allowed to cross the halls' imposing inner court between 8.00 a.m. and 6.00 p.m. during the week, and between 9.00 a.m. and 6.00 p.m. on Saturday. The Markt is at the other end of the yard. If the gate is closed, turn back and walk down Hallestraat, which runs parallel to the Halls.

Walk 2 (see pages 45-47) comments extensively on Markt.

Return to the Belfry **05** and walk down Breidelstraat, a traffic-free alley on the corner. Continue to Burg.

Along the way on your right you will notice De Garre, a narrow alley. This may be the narrowest street in Bruges (try walking side by side here!), it nevertheless boasts a fair number of cosy cafés. Burg is the most majestic square in the city, so take your time to admire its grandeur. The main character in this medieval story is the City Hall **09** **43** (1376-1420), one of the oldest city halls in the Netherlands and a Gothic example for all its brothers and sisters that were built later, from Louvain to Audenarde and Brussels. Having admired its exterior, enter the impressive Gothic Hall and gaze in admiration at the

BURG: AN ARCHITECTURAL SYNOPSIS

Art lovers have already noticed that Burg projects a wonderful cross-section of stunning architectural styles. It is, indeed, a summing-up in one place of all the styles that have caught our imagination throughout the various centuries. From Romanesque (Saint Basil's Church) and Gothic (City Hall) by way of Renaissance (Civil Registry) and Baroque (Deanery) to Classicism (Mansion of the Liberty of Bruges). There's no need to go and dash all around Bruges to see it all!

01

polychrome floating ribs of the vaulted ceiling. Hiding on the right-hand side of this Gothic monument is the Basilica of the Holy Blood **01**. It was originally dedicated to both Our Lady and Saint Basil, and was built as a fortress church on two levels between 1139 and 1157. The lower church, hidden away behind the Gothic Saint Ivo's Chapel, has retained its Romanesque character. The upper chapel, which was originally little more than a kind of balcony, was gradually extended over the years to become a church in its own right. It was only during the 19th century that it was renovated in the neo-Gothic style that can be seen today. The sacred relic of the Holy Blood has been kept here since the 13th century. Each year on Ascension Day, the reliquary is carried along in the Procession of the Holy Blood, a much-loved event that has been warming the hearts of the entire population from as early as 1304. Facing the basilica is the gleaming Renais-

sance façade of the erstwhile Civil Registry **03** (1534-1537, which now houses the City Archive **08**) adjacent to the Liberty of Bruges **01** **15**. Its showpiece is a splendid oak mantelpiece with an alabaster frieze (1529). Adjoining is the former mansion of the Liberty of Bruges (1722-1727). It is from here that the country around Bruges was administered. After 1795 a court of justice was installed. It has been the city's administrative centre since 1988. Once upon a time Saint Donatian's Cathedral graced the spot directly in front of the City Hall. The church was torn down in 1799. Adjacent to it is the Deanery (1655-1666) **17**. It is still possible to see the foundations of parts of the old cathedral in the cellar of the Crown Plaza Hotel.

Fishy stories

Proceed to Blinde-Ezelstraat, the little street to the left of the City Hall. Don't forget to look back at the lovely arch between City Hall and Old Civil Registry **03** **08**. Do you see Solomon? Left of him is the statue of Prosperity, to the right the statue of Peace.
According to tradition, Blinde-Ezelstraat (Blind Donkey Street) owes its name to a tavern of the same name. The house in the left hand corner hugging the water used to house a mill driven by a donkey. In order to preserve the poor animal from the depressing thought that the only thing it had to do

purpose in 1821, fresh seafood was sold, a delicacy that only the rich could afford. Today you can still buy your fresh saltwater fish here every morning from Tuesday to Saturday.

Retrace your steps and turn left in front of the bridge towards Huidenvettersplein.

Whereas Vismarkt served the rich, Huidenvettersplein (Tanners Square) served the poor. No sea fish on the menu here, but affordable freshwater fish. The post in the middle of the square used to have a twin brother: in between the two posts hung the scales that the fish were weighed on. The large, striking building dominating the square used to be the meeting hall of the tanners. Here they sold the cow hides that they had turned into leather. Since tanning was a rather smelly job, it is no coincidence that the tanners' hall adjoined the fish market. Look out for

was turn endless rounds, a blindfold was put on its head. A new street name was born. Look left on the bridge: Meebrug is said to be the oldest bridge in Bruges.

Vismarkt **22** opens up immediately past the bridge.

At first, fish was sold on one of the Markt's corners, but as the townspeople complained about the stench, the fishmongers were forced to move and sell their wares here. In the covered arcade, specially erected for the

Huidenvettersplein

the statuette adorning the corner of the hall. It is no surprise that the little fellow raises his nose.

Continue to Rozenhoedkaai. Keep right.
Rozenhoedkaai is the most photographed spot in Bruges. So, take out your camera! This used to be the salt port. In the Middle Ages salt was as expensive as gold: it served to preserve food and to season dishes. A word like *salaris* (Dutch), *salaire* (French), *salary* still harks back to medieval times. The word derives from *sal*, which is Latin for salt.

From Groeninge to the Bonifacius Bridge

Continue along Dijver.
In the middle of the 11th century, the hermit Everelmus built a prayer chapel on Dijver. Along this atmospheric stretch of water, you will first find the College of Europe (numbers 9 to 11) **03**, an international postgraduate institution that focuses on European affairs, and then the Groeninge Museum **27**, Bruges' most renowned museum. On display are world-famous masterpieces by Jan van Eyck, Hans Memling, Hugo van der Goes, Gerard David and many other Flemish primitives. The museum also has a valuable collection of Flemish expressionists, neoclassical top notch paintings from the 18th and 19th centuries and post-war modern art. Overall, the museum shows a complete overview of Belgian and southern Dutch (Flemish) painting from the 15th to the 20th century. The museum entrance is reached through a few picturesque courtyard gardens.

ALMSHOUSES, THE QUICKEST WAY TO HEAVEN

These charitable dwellings were built from the 14th century onwards. They were sometimes set up by the guilds to lodge their elderly members, and sometimes by widows or well-to-do burghers who wanted to ensure their place in heaven. In order to secure their spot, each set of

almshouses had its own chapel, in which the inhabitants were morally obliged to offer prayers of thanks to heaven. Practically all of the almshouses have been carefully restored and modernised and offer cosy living to today's elderly, whilst their small yet picturesque gardens and white-painted façades offer welcoming peace and quiet to the present-day visitor. Feel free to enter these premises, but don't forget to respect their perfect tranquillity.

(On the City map the Almshouses are indicated by 🏠.)

Would you like to find out more about the Flemish primitives? Then leaf through to the interview on pages 112-115 with Till-Holger Borchert, the Groeninge Museum's chief curator.

Continue along Dijver. The entrance gate to the Gruuthuse Museum **28** is on your left just beyond the little bridge. This museum is closed for restoration until 2018.

Continue to Guido Gezelleplein, then turn left in front of the Church of Our Lady **15** **35** and follow the narrow footpath to the picturesque Bonifacius Bridge. Due to renovation works, it is possible that the footpath will be closed for a time. If this is the case, follow the alternative route as indicated on the map (dotted line).

The crosses that you see all over the place don't belong to graves at all – they are crosses taken down from church steeples during the First World War to disorientate the enemy spies. The crosses have never been put up again.

Close to the Bonifacius Bridge is Bruges' smallest Gothic window. Look up! It was through this window that the lords and ladies of Gruuthuse were able to peer down onto their private jetty. Across the bridge is the charming city garden Hof Arents of the Arentshuis **03**, an elegant 18th-century abode. The top floor houses work by the versatile British artist Frank Brangwyn. The ground floor is reserved for temporary exhibitions. Rik Poot's (1924-2006) remarkable sculpture group in the garden represents the *Horsemen of the Apocalypse*: famine, death, revolution and the plague. A theme that appealed to the painter Hans Memling as well. Go through the garden gate to reach the Groeninge Museum **27**, where more work by Memling is displayed.

On to the Beguinage!

Leave the garden once more through the narrow garden gate and turn left into Groeninge, a winding street. Turn right again at the intersection with Nieuwe Gentweg. Notice the Saint

Joseph and the De Meulenaere 🏠 almshouses (both from the 17th century). Continue down the street. On the left-hand corner of Oude Gent-weg and Katelijnestraat is the Diamond Museum **21**, Bruges' most glittering museum and the place to be for all lovers of bling. It goes without saying that an inspiring diamond museum simply couldn't be absent in the most romantic city of the western hemisphere!

Wijngaardplein

Turn left into Katelijnestraat, then immediately right into Wijngaardstraat. Cross Wijngaardplein – a stopping place for coachmen. A little further on turn right onto the bridge beside the Sashuis (lock house) to enter the Beguinage. The bridge offers a fine view of the Minnewater.

The Minnewater used to be the landing stage of the barges or track boats that provided a regular connection between Bruges and Ghent. Today it is one of Bruges' most romantic beauty spots. Equally atmospheric, yet of a totally different nature, is the Beguinage. Although the 'Princely Beguinage Ten Wijngaarde' **02** **02**, founded in 1245, is no longer occupied by beguines (single lay women who formed their own religious community), but by nuns of the Order of Saint Benedict, you can still form an excellent picture of what daily life looked like in the 17th century at the Beguine's house **04**. The imposing courtyard garden, the white painted house fronts and blessed peace create

an atmosphere all of its own. The entrance gates are closed each day at 6.30 p.m. without fail.

Walk around the Beguinage and leave through the main gate. Turn left after the bridge and left again to reach Walplein.

De Halve Maan **12**, a brewery established as early as 1564, is at number 26 (at your left hand side). This is Bruges' last active city brewery. Their speciality is *Brugse Zot* (Bruges' Fool), a spirited top-fermented beer made from malt, hop and special yeast. The name of the

02

beer refers to the nickname of the Bruges townspeople, a name allegedly conferred upon them by Maximilian of Austria. In order to welcome the duke, the citizens paraded past him in a lavish procession of brightly coloured merrymakers and fools. When a short time later they asked their ruler to finance a new 'zothuis' or madhouse, his answer was as short as it was forceful: *'The only people I have seen here are fools. Bruges is one big madhouse. Just close the gates.'*

A splendid finish at Saint John's Hospital

Turn left into Zonnekemeers. Once across the water, turn right to enter the area of Old Saint John via the car park.

The former Hospital of Saint John (13th-14th centuries) **39** has a proud eight century-long history. The oldest documents even date back to the 12th century! Here, nuns and monks took good care of pilgrims, travellers and the sick. And people sometimes chose to die here. Hans Memling once was a patient here too. According to a much later legend, he rewarded his benefactors with no fewer than six masterpieces. Right in front of the convent buildings of the old hospital complex you will come across *The Veins of the Convent*, a sculptural work by the contemporary Italian artist Giuseppe Penone. Or how history still feeds the

present – what could be more appropriate for a World Heritage City like Bruges! Turn left at the corner and then go immediately right: in the open space of the courtyard you will find the herb garden and the entrance to the 17th century pharmacy, which is well worth a visit. The herb garden contains all the necessary ingredients for 'gruut' or 'gruit', including lady's mantle, myrtle and laurel. You can find an explanation of what gruut is in *walk 2 on page 44*. Retrace your steps, turn left and walk through the passage. The entrance to the imposing medieval hospital wards, its chapel, the Diksmuide attic and the old dormitory are just around the corner to the right.

Walk 2
Bruges, a Burgundian city

When, during Bruges' Golden Age Philip the Bold, Duke of Burgundy, married Margaret of Dampierre, the daughter of the last Count of Flanders, the county of Flanders suddenly found itself belonging to Burgundy. As the Burgundian court liked to stay in Bruges, the port city became a magnet for noblemen, merchants and artists. They naturally all wanted to get their share of the city's wealth. Today the Burgundian influence is still strongly felt throughout Bruges. Let's discover a northern city with a southern character.

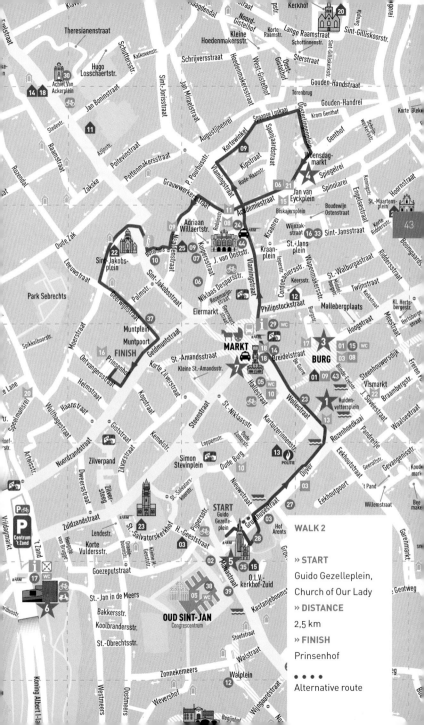

WALK 2

» START

Guido Gezelleplein,
Church of Our Lady

» DISTANCE

2,5 km

» FINISH

Prinsenhof

•••••
Alternative route

From Guido Gezelleplein to Markt

This square is named after the Flemish-priest and poet Guido Gezelle (1830-1899). Take a seat on one of the square's benches and enjoy Gezelle's lovely statue and the side-view of the Church of Our Lady 15 35. Its one hundred and fifteen (and a half!)-metre high brick tower is sure proof of the craftsmanship of Bruges' artisans. The church is currently undergoing largescale renovation work, so that it is not possible to admire all its many fine works of art. However, Michelangelo's world-famous *Madonna and Child* can still be viewed. On your left is the striking residence of the lords of Gruuthuse, now the Gruuthuse Museum 28. This, too, is undergoing renovation works and will be closed until 2018. The tower and well (which unfortunately cannot be seen from the Guido Gezelleplein) were status symbols, and evidence of the Gruuthuse family's great wealth. They made their fortune

from their exclusive rights on 'gruut', a herb mixture that, ages before hop, was used to flavour beer. Louis of Gruuthuse not only commanded the army of Charles the Bold, he was also the personal bodyguard to Mary of Burgundy. A cultured man, he owned the Gruuthuse manuscript, a famous medieval codex containing amongst its many texts no fewer than 147 songs. The family's motto was *Plus est en vous* (There is more in you than you think). It's proudly displayed above the door of their residence.

Continue along the narrow footpath to the left of the church. Due to renovation works, it is possible that this footpath will not be accessible.
Look up immediately beyond the bend. Do you see the chapel that seems to hold the Gruuthuse Museum and the Church of Our Lady in a close embrace? As the lords of Gruuthuse were far too grand to mingle with the populace, they had their own private chapel high above the street, where they could follow Mass. This intimate place of worship can still be visited.

Retrace your steps, cross the attractive Gruuthuseplein and turn right into Dijver.
Number 12 is the Groeninge Museum 27 , Bruges' most famous museum. *An interview with chief curator Till-Holger Borchert is on pages 112-115.*
Further along Dijver is one of the locations of the College of Europe 03 , numbers 9-11, an international post-graduate institution that focuses on Europe.

Carry on down Dijver and turn left into Wollestraat.
Perez de Malvenda 13 is an impressive mansion on the corner of Wollestraat. This 15th-16th century town house, now a food shop, has been restored from attic to cellar. Just before Markt are the Cloth Halls 10 , the Belfry's 05 warehouses and sales outlets. Facing the street, countless stalls were selling all sorts of herbs for medicinal purpose and potions. Indeed, Bruges being an important trading centre could by then import and sell a variety of herbs from all over Europe.

Markt, Bruges' beating heart

Wollestraat leads to Markt.
Markt is dominated by its Belfry 05 , for centuries the city's foremost edifice and the perfect lookout in case of war, fire or any other calamity. You can still climb to the top of the tower; but you will need to conquer no fewer than 366 steps to get there! Fortunately, there are a couple of places during your

THE RIGHT TIME

On the market square (Markt), at the very top of the late-Gothic corner house 'Bouchoute', which is currently home to the Meridian 3 tearoom, there is a shining ball decorated with gold leaf. At the time of the inauguration of the Brussels-Ghent-Bruges railway line, people were aware that the clocks in Belgium did not all keep the same time. This problem was solved in Bruges in 1837 by Professor Quetelet, who 'drew' a meridian on the ground and set up a noonday 'hand' that would show incontestably when it was twelve o'clock. This meridian ran diagonally over the Markt and is now marked by a series of copper nails. When the shadow of the golden ball falls on the meridian, it is midday precisely: 12.00 p.m. local solar time.

Markt

ascent where you can stop for a breather. Once at the top you will be rewarded with an unforgettable panoramic view. At the foot of the Belfry are the world's most famous chippies ('frietkoten')! The statue of Jan Breydel and Pieter de Coninck graces the middle of the square. These two popular heroes of Bruges resisted French oppression and consequently played an important part during the Battle of the Golden Spurs in 1302. Their statue neatly looks out onto

TIP

As you are climbing your way to the top of the belfry tower, why not stop for a break at the vaulted treasure chamber, where the city's charters, seal and public funds were all kept during medieval times. You can make a second stop at the 'Stenen Vloer' (Stone Floor): here you will learn everything you ever wanted to know about the clock, the

drum and the carillon of 47 harmonious bells, which together weigh a staggering 27 tons of pure bronze. If you are really lucky, you might see the carilloneur in action, banging on the wooden keys that make the bells sound.

the Gothic revival style Provincial Court (Markt 3) . Until the 18th century this was the place – now occupied by the Post Office, the Historium and the Bruges Beer Museum – where proudly stood the Water Halls (Waterhalle), a covered warehouse where goods were loaded and unloaded along the river Reie that ran alongside the square. Today the river is still there, but now runs through a series of underground vaults. Would you like a break? Then treat yourself to a coach ride and explore the city by horse and carriage for half an hour (see page 71). Or maybe you prefer a fifty-minute city tour by minibus (see page 71)? You can continue your walk after your trip.

From Markt to Jan van Eyckplein

Keep Markt on your left and continue straight ahead to Vlamingstraat.
In the 13th century, this used to be the harbour area's shopping street. A fair number of banks had a branch here, and wine taverns were two a penny. Each of these had (and still has) a deep cellar where French and Rhenish wines could easily be stacked. In the medieval vaulted cellars of Taverne Curiosa (Vlamingstraat 22), the alcoholic atmosphere of those bygone days can still be inhaled. Halfway along Vlamingstraat is the elegant City Theatre on your left. This royal theatre (1869) is one of Europe's best-preserved city theatres. Behind the Neo-Renaissance façade lie a magnificent auditorium and a

---

TIP

Since as long ago as 1897, two green painted mobile chippies have stood in front of the Belfry. It is definitely the best place in town to buy – and sell – chips, good for the annual consumption of several tons of fast food! The city's chip-sellers can bid once every two years for the right to stand on this lucrative spot. The highest bidder gets the contract. The stalls are open nearly every hour of the day and night, so that you never need to go hungry!

Vlamingstraat

SWANS ON THE CANALS

After the death of Mary of Burgundy (1482), Bruges went through some troubled times. The townspeople, enraged by new taxes Maximilian of Austria, Mary's successor, had imposed upon them, rose in revolt against their new ruler. As Maximilian was locked up in

House Craenenburg on the market square, he helplessly witnessed the torture and eventual beheading of his bailiff and trusted councillor Pieter Lanchals (Long Neck). A deep-rooted legend claims that, once the duke had regained power, the citizens of Bruges were ordered to keep swans or long necks ('langhalzen') on the canals for all eternity. In fact, swans were already swimming in the moats around Bruges at the beginning of the 15th century.

palatial foyer. Papageno, the bird seller from Mozart's opera, *The Magic Flute*, guards the entrance. His score lies scattered on the square opposite.

Continue along Vlamingstraat and turn right into Kortewinkel just before the water.

Somewhat hidden from gazing eyes, Kortewinkel boasts a unique 16th-century wooden house front. It is one of only two left in the city (you will come across the other one further along this walk). Just a few metres on is another delicious discovery at number 10. The Jesuit House **09** has a magnificent hidden courtyard garden. Is its door open? Then walk in and enjoy its heavenly peace.

Kortewinkel turns into Spaanse Loskaai, the home port of the Spanish merchants until the end of the 16th century.

The picturesque bridge on your left is the Augustine Bridge, one of Bruges' oldest specimens, with its seven hundred summers. The stone seats were originally intended to display the wares of the diligent sellers. The bridge affords an excellent view of the house in the right-hand corner, which connects Spanjaardstraat with Kortewinkel. This was once the House of God's Succour but is also said to be a haunted house, according to the locals. When an amorous monk was rejected by a nun, the man murdered her and then committed suicide. Ever since they have been haunting that ramshackle building...

Continue along Spaanse Loskaai, go down the first street on your right and proceed to Oosterlingenplein.
During Bruges' Golden Age this was the fixed abode of the so-called 'Oosterlingen' (Easteners) or German merchants. Their imposing warehouse took up the entire left side of the square. Today the only remnant is the building to the right of Hotel Bryghia. Their warehouse must have been truly grand!

Beyond Oosterlingenplein is Woensdagmarkt. You will then find yourself on the square on which the statue of the painter Hans Memling attracts all attention. Turn right into Genthof.
Here the second of two authentic medieval wooden house fronts draws attention. Notice that each floor juts out a little more than the next one. This building technique, which helped to avoid water damage (but also created extra space), was consequently used in various architectural styles.

Burgundian Manhattan

Proceed to Jan van Eyckplein.
This was Burgundian Bruges' Manhattan, the place to be! Here ships docked, cargoes were loaded and unloaded and tolls were levied. In this unremitting hustle and bustle a cacophony of languages was heard above the din, the one sounding even louder than the other. What a soundtrack! Each business transaction required a few local sounds too, of course, as there always had to be a Bruges broker present who would naturally pocket his cut. On the corner, the 16th-century Huis De Rode Steen (number 8) has been sparkling in all its glory since its restoration (the first building in Bruges to be renovated thanks to a subsidy from the city) in 1877. At numbers 1-2 is the Old Tollhouse (1477) **06 21**, where all tollage was settled. To the left of this monumental building is Pijndershuisje, Bruges' narrowest dwelling. This is where the 'pijnders' or dock-workers used to meet. You can guess the origin of the name by looking at the facade; but

> TIP
>
> The Genthof has in recent years attracted a variety of different arts and crafts. There is a glass-blower, a trendy vintage store and a number of contemporary art galleries. And on the corner you can find 't Terrastje, the café with probably the smallest terrace in Bruges.

you need to look carefully! The hunched 'pijnders' were employed to load and unload sacks and casks.

Continue along Academiestraat.
Right on the corner with Jan van Eyck-plein is another remarkable building, distinguished by its striking tower. This is the Poortersloge (Burghers' Lodge) 15 , a 15th-century building where the burgesses of the city (patricians and merchants) once used to meet. In a wall niche, the Bruges Bear, an important city symbol, stands proud and upright. From 1720 to 1890, the Burghers' Lodge housed the Municipal Academy of Fine Arts. From 1912 to 2012, the building served as the home of the State Archives.

Proceed to Grauwwerkersstraat.
The little square connecting Acade-miestraat with Grauwwerkersstraat has been known as 'Beursplein' since time immemorial.

Here merchants were engaged in high-quality trade. The merchant houses of Genoa (Genuese Lodge, later renamed 'Saaihalle' 08 , and today Belgian Fries Museum 24), Florence (now De Floren-tijnen restaurant) and Venice once stood here side by side like brothers. In front of Huis ter Beurze (1276), the central inn 11 , merchants from all over Europe used to gather to arrange business appointments and conduct exchange transactions. The Dutch word for stock exchange became 'beurs', derived from the name of the house. Many other languages would take over this term, such as French (bourse) or Italian (borsa).

Turn into Grauwwerkersstraat and stop immediately in your tracks.
The side wall of Huis ter Beurze 11 , and more precisely the part between

THE LITTLE BEAR OF BRUGES

When Baldwin Iron Arm, the first Count of Flanders, visited Bruges for the first time, the first creature he saw was a big 'white' bear. According to the legend, all this happened in the 9th century. After a fierce fight the count succeeded in killing the animal. In homage to the courageous beast, he proclaimed the bear to be the city's very own symbol. Today 'Bruges' oldest inhabitant' in the niche of the Burghers' Lodge is festively rigged out during exceptional celebrations. The Bruges Bear is holding the coat of arms of the Noble Company of the White Bear, which was a kind of jousting club for local knights, founded shortly after Baldwin's famous victory over the original 'white' bear.

the two sets of ground-floor windows, bears the signatures of the stonecutters. This way everybody knew which mason cut which stones and how much each mason had to be paid. The house next-door to Huis ter Beurze, called 'de Kleine Beurze' (the Little Beurze), still sits on its original street level.

Turn left into Naaldenstraat. On your right, Bladelin Court 09 with its attractive tower looms up ahead. In the 15th century, Pieter Bladelin, portrayed above the gate whilst praying to the Virgin Mary, leased his house to the Florentine banking family of de' Medici, who set up one of their branches here. Today the edifice belongs to the Sisters of Our Lady of Seven Sorrows. We highly recommend a visit. But make a reservation before you go *[see pages 85-86]* and admire the magnificent courtyard garden and the city's first Renaissance façade, embellished with two stone medallions representing Lorenzo de' Medici and his wife Clarissa Orsini.

08 11 24

PRINSENHOF GOSSIP

> As Philip the Good hadn't yet laid eyes on his future wife, he sent Jan van Eyck to Portugal to paint her portrait. This way the duke wanted to make certain he had made the right choice. The duke's ploy worked, because history teaches us that the couple had a happy marriage.

> Although the popular Mary of Burgundy incurred only seemingly minor injuries as a result of a fall with her horse, the accident would eventually lead to her death from a punctured lung at Prinsenhof. Back in those times there was no cure for inflammation.

> During the hotel renovation no fewer than 568 silver coins, minted between 1755 and 1787, were dug up. After some careful counting and calculations it is assumed that the energetic English nuns, who lived there at that time, entrusted the coins to the soil so as to prevent the advancing French troops from stealing their hard-earned capital.

Somewhat further along, next to another ornamental tower, turn right into Boterhuis, a winding cobbled alley that catapults you back straight into the Middle Ages. Keep right, pass Saint James' Church and turn left into Moerstraat.

The Dukes of Burgundy and the vast majority of foreign merchants patronised Saint Jacob's Church **22**. Their extravagant gifts have left their glittering mark on the interior.

Prinsenhof (the Princes' Court), home base of the Dukes of Burgundy

Turn left into Geerwijnstraat and carry on to Muntplein.

Muntplein (Coin Square) belongs to nearby Prinsenhof **16**. As you might have guessed, this was where Bruges' mint was situated. The statue *Flandria Nostra* (Our Flanders), which represents a noblewoman on horseback, was designed by the Belgian sculptor Jules Lagae (1862-1931).

Muntpoort

At the end of Geerwijnstraat turn right into Geldmuntstraat. The walk's finishing point is Prinsenhof.

We end the walk on a highlight. Prinsenhof used to be the palace of the Flemish counts and Burgundy dukes. This impressive mansion, originally seven times the size of what you see today, was erected in the 15th century by Philip the Good to celebrate his (third) marriage to Isabella of Portugal. When Charles the Bold remarried Margaret of York, the largest bathhouse in Europe, a game court (to play 'jeu de paume' or the palm game, the forerunner of tennis) and a zoological garden were all added to the ducal residence. It is no surprise that Prinsenhof not only became the favourite pied-à-terre of

TIP

Whoever wants to get a really good impression of the magnificence of this city castle and its elegant gardens should follow the signs in the Ontvangersstraat to the hotel car park at Moerstraat 46. Of course, you can always treat yourself – and your nearest and dearest – to a princely drink in the bar of the hotel: the perfect way to enjoy the grandeur and luxury of the complex.

the Dukes of Burgundy, but also the nerve centre of their political, economic and cultural ambitions. Both Philip the Good (d.1467) and Mary of Burgundy (d.1482) breathed their last here. After the death of the popular Mary of Burgundy the palace's fortunes declined, until it eventually ended up in private hands. In the 17th century, English nuns converted it into a boarding school for girls of well-to-do parents. Nowadays you can stay in the Prinsenhof Castle in true princely style.

TIP

Behind the street Boterhuis, at Sint-Jakobsstraat 26, you will find Cinema Lumière **10**, purveyor of the better kind of artistic film. In other words, the place to be for real film-lovers.

Walk 3
Strolling through silent Bruges

Although the parishes of Saint Anne and Saint Giles are known as places of great tranquillity, the fact that they are off the beaten track does not mean that the visitor will be short of adventure. How about a row of nostalgic windmills? Or perhaps some unpretentious working-class neighbourhoods or a couple of exclusive gentlemen's clubs? Will you be able to absorb all these impressions serenely? Don't worry. After the tour we invite you to catch your breath in Bruges' oldest cafe!

DAMPOORT

55

WALK 3

» **START**
Choco-Story
(Wijnzakstraat 2)

» **DISTANCE**
4 km

» **FINISH**
Café Vlissinghe
(Blekersstraat 2)

From Choco-Story to Gouden-Handstraat

Choco-Story (Chocolate Museum) **16** is the perfect starting point for the longest walk in this guide. This museum not only dips you in the yummy history of chocolate and cocoa, it also offers extensive chocolate tasting. If you wish, you can also buy your supplies here. No doubt the chocolate will help you to keep up a brisk pace! At the same address Lumina Domestica **33** contains the world's largest collection of lamps and lights. The museum also houses 6,000 antiques.

Turn left into Sint-Jansstraat, carry on to Korte Riddersstraat and continue until the end of the street.
Saint Walburga's Church **24** rises up in all its magnificence right in front of you. This Baroque edifice (1619-1642) boasts a remarkable marble communion rail and high altar. Nearby, at number 3 there is a splendid 18th century mansion.

Continue down Koningstraat to the bridge.
This bridge, which connects poetic Spinolarei with Spiegelrei, affords a lovely view of Oud Huis Amsterdam on your left. Today this historic town house (Spiegelrei 3) is an elegant hotel. This part of the city used to be mainly populated by the English and Scots. The English merchants even had their own 'steegere' or stair where their goods were unloaded. The stair is still there, and the street connecting it is appropriately called Engelsestraat. The dignified white school building (number 15) across the bridge was once a college of English Jesuits.

Saint Giles', home base of workmen and artists

Cross the bridge, turn right along Spiegelrei and turn into Gouden-Handstraat, the fourth street on your left.
In the 15th century Gouden-Handstraat and the parish of Saint Giles were known as the artists' quarter. Hans Memling may have lived a few streets further down in Sint-Jorisstraat; the fact of the matter is that Jan van Eyck had a studio in Gouden-Handstraat, and that his somewhat lesser known

fellow artists also used to congregate in this neighbourhood.

Turn right into Sint-Gilliskerkstraat. This street bumps into Saint Giles' Church **20** in the heart of the tranquil quarter of Saint Giles'. Initially a chapel, this building was upgraded to a parish church in 1258. In spite of its interior in Gothic revival style and its superb paintings, the church takes on the appearance of a simple, sturdy village church. Don't be misled. In and around the church countless famous painters were buried, such as Hans Memling (d.1494), in his time the best-paid painter, Lanceloot Blondeel (d.1561) and Pieter Pourbus (d.1584). Their graves and the cemetery may have disappeared, but their artists' souls still hover in the air.

Walk around the church and turn into Sint-Gilliskoorstraat.

Although the workmen's dwellings in these streets are rather small, they nevertheless display a bricked up window. As it happened, a tax on windows was levied in 1800. As a consequence, a large number of windows were walled up.

From Potterierei to the vesten (ramparts)

Turn left into Langerei at the end of the street. Cross the lovely Snaggaardbrug, the first bridge you get to, into Potterierei. Turn left and follow the canal for some time.

After a fair distance along Potterierei is Bruges' Major Seminary (num-

Woensdagmarkt

20

BRUGES AND THE SEA

For centuries, Potterierei ensured the city's wealth. This canal ran to Damme where it was connected to a large lock, called 'Speie', which in turn was connected to the Zwin, a deep sea channel and tidal inlet. While Damme developed into an outport, Bruges grew into Northwestern Europe's greatest business centre of the Middle Ages. The arts flourished, culture thrived, prosperity seemed to be set for all eternity. The tide turned when Mary of Burgundy suddenly passed away in 1482. The relations between Bruges and the Burgundians turned sour and the Burgundian court left the city. The foreign merchants and their wealth followed in its wake. The Zwin continued to silt up and Bruges lost her privileged commercial position. As a result, and compounded by a series of political intrigues, the city fell into a deep winter sleep.

ber 72) **05** on your right. A unique place with a lush orchard and meadows with cows at pasture. Between 1628 and 1642 a new Cistercian Abbey (the Dune Abbey) was erected here, which later on would achieve great fame for the wealth and erudition of its occupants. During the French Revolution, the abbey was brought under public ownership, and the abbot and monks were chased away. The 17th-century abbey buildings were first used as a military hospital and then as a military depot and a grammar school before they were eventually taken over by the Major Seminary in 1833. Up to the present day the Seminary has been training Catholic priests here. Just a few yards further down at number 79B is Our Lady of the Pottery **16** **36**. Its history goes back to the 13th century. Diligent nuns used to treat pilgrims, travellers and the sick here. From the 15th century onwards, it also became a home for the care of the elderly. The Gothic church with its Baroque interior and its rich collection of works of art, accumulated by the hospital throughout the centuries, is a hidden gem that is certainly well worth a visit!

05

Carry on to the lock and spend some time by the water.

This idyllic spot is where the canal Damse Vaart heads out across the other side of the ring road towards the equally romantic town of Damme. It's hard to believe that this area around the canal was once a scene of great controversy. Up until the Eighty Years' War, Bruges was connected to Sluis by way of Damme. Ambitious Napoleon Bonaparte had the link with the tidal inlet of the Zwin, the natural predecessor of the Damse Vaart, dredged by Spanish prisoners of war so as to create a watercourse that would run all the way to Antwerp. His plan then was to develop the port city of Antwerp into a naval base, which would enable him to avoid the English sea blockade. Napoleon's project left Damme cut in twain. The wild plans of the little general were never carried out in full, and by 1815 Napole-

TIP

Have we made you curious? Or do you just like to do things the easy way? If so, leave your bike and car at home and 'all aboard' for a voyage on the Lamme Goedzak 🚃, the most stylish way to reach the town of Damme. Step back in time during this nostalgic journey. *(For more information see pages 67-68.)*

on's role in Flanders had come to an end. However, the Dutch King William I also saw the 'benefits' of a connecting canal, and so excavation work was continued until 1824. Belgian independence (1830) meant that the project was finally terminated, by which time it had reached as far as Sluis. Today the low-traffic bicycle path skirting the canal is a most attractive route linking Bruges with Damme. The trip is highly recom-

Sasplein

THE ARCHERS' GUILD:
120 MEN AND 2 QUEENS!

Two centuries-old archery clubs are now to be found in what for many years was one of the poorer districts of Bruges. High and dry on the same hill as the Sint-Janshuis Mill, at the bottom left, stands the Sint-Joris (St. George's) Guild **41**, a crossbow guild that specializes in two archery disciplines: shooting 'the feather' and shooting at targets. To the right, with its eye-catching target tower, is the home of the Sint-Sebastiaan (St. Sebastian) Guild **42**, a longbow society. This guild goes back more than six centuries, which makes it unique in the world. The society numbers 120 male members exactly and two notable female honorary members: the Belgian queen Mathilde and the British queen. Ever since the exiled English king Charles II took up residence in Bruges in the 17ᵗʰ century, the city and the British Royal Family have always been closely associated. Whenever the British Royal Family is on a state visit to Belgium, so the rumour goes, they first of all pop in at the Saint Sebastian's Archers' Guild.

mended, as it traverses *le plat pays*, that flat country made famous by Jacques Brel in the moving song of that name. Imagine! In the middle of a unique polder landscape this truly poetic canal strip, bordered by lofty poplars bended down by eternal westerly winds.

Turn right and carry on along the Vesten (canals), which surround the city like a ring of green.
In the 16ᵗʰ century, more than thirty windmills were turning their sails here. Today only four are left. In the 18ᵗʰ century, the millers stood by helplessly when bread consumption took a dive

and people started to consume more potatoes. Eventually steam machines would take over the millers' tasks. One of the mills, the Sint-Janshuis Mill **40** can still be visited today. A miller not only provides expert explanation, but also shows you how to grind grain. The Koelewei Mill **32** is closed until 2017 because of renovation works. Make sure you climb the slopes on which the Sint-Janshuis Mill and the Bonne Chiere Mill (just next to the Kruispoort/Cross Gate **12**) proudly stand! The hills afford a fantastic panoramic view of the city. This is the perfect spot to brush up on your amassed knowl-

edge of Bruges. And there's more! Down below on your right is the Verloren Hoek (the Lost Corner), now an authentic working-class district, but back in the 19th century an impoverished neighbourhood with such a bad reputation that even the police didn't dare enter its streets.

TIP

Interested in a little something 'extra'? Then go and take a look at the Albrecht Rodenbachstraat, another of the city's hidden gems. This green suburb avant la lettre offers an almost unbroken succession of stepgables and other fascinating facades, each fronted by a delightful little garden.

Silent Bruges

Descend down the slope and turn right into Rolweg.

Right on the corner is the Gezelle Museum 26, the birthplace of Guido Gezelle (1830-1899), one of Flanders' most venerable poets. On display are handwritten letters, writing material and a deliciously peaceful garden with an age-old Corsican pine. Gezelle's parents worked here as gardener and caretaker, in exchange for which they and their family received free board and lodging. Little Guido grew up in these idyllic surroundings. He would eventually return to Bruges many years later and after many a peregrination. Upon his return he became curate of Saint Walburga's Church 24. He also took over the running of the English Convent 04 (Carmersstraat 83-85), where he would die. These were his last words, reportedly: 'I have so loved hearing the *birds singing.'* Here, in this most verdant part of Bruges, we still know precisely what the priest and poet meant.

Turn into Balstraat, the second street on the left.
This picturesque working-man's alley houses the Folklore Museum (Volkskundemuseum) **45**. The 17th-century row of single-room dwellings, restored and converted into authentic artisans' interiors such as a milliner's, a confectioner's and a small classroom, will take you back to bygone days. The tower of the 15th-century Jerusalem Chapel **08** can easily be spotted from these premises. This chapel was commissioned by the Adornes, a prominent Bruges merchant family of Genovese origin, who lived in a

TIP

If you feel like taking a break, you are welcome to rest your tired feet in the large, walled garden of the Folklore Museum. It is a delightful oasis of calm in the heart of the city, and even has its own outdoor pétanque alley!

magnificent mansion **01** on the Peperstraat. In 1470 Anselm Adornes collected one of his sons (the father had no fewer than sixteen children) in Padua to set off on a pilgrimage to the Holy Land. Upon his return to Bruges, Anselm decided to build an exact copy of the Church of the Holy Sepulchre. The result was remarkable. In the adjacent Adornes Estate **01**,

you will make closer acquaintance with this prominent family and its intriguing history. Around the corner, at Balstraat 16, you can visit the new Lace Centre , which has been installed in the fully renovated old lace School. If you visit during one of the many lace demonstrations (2.00-5.00 p.m., not on Sunday and public holidays), it is almost like stepping back in time.

At the crossroads turn right into Jeruzalemstraat; then, at the church, left unto Sint-Annaplein.
The tiny square is dominated by the apparently simple Church of Saint Anne **19**. Its exterior may be austere, but its interior is one of Bruges' most splendid examples of Baroque architecture. As

this neighbourhood gradually became more prestigious, the church did the same!

With the church behind you follow the Sint-Annakerkstraat and then turn right into Sint-Annarei.
At the corner of the confluence of the two waterways one of Bruges' most handsome town houses is proudly showing off its Rococo credentials (Sint-Annarei no. 22). Sit yourself down on a shady bench and enjoy this exceptional prospect.

Retrace your steps for just a few yards and turn left into Blekersstraat next to the bridge.
Café Vlissinghe at number 2 is undoubtedly Bruges' oldest café. This has been a tavern since 1515. It is no surprise then that you will find oodles of ambiance here. It is therefore the perfect place to settle down and let the wonderful memories of your walk slowly sink in. A local beer will be your ideal companion. Cheers!

Café Vlissinghe

Know your way around
Bruges

Exploring Bruges

You might want to stroll, amble and saunter down the streets of Bruges all day long. However, why not try to see the city from a different perspective? During a walking or bicycle tour, a guide will show you numerous secret places. Maybe you would prefer a boat trip on the mysterious canals – an unforgettable experience! And a ride in a horse-drawn carriage must surely be the perfect romantic outing. Sport-lovers can even do a guided run around the city. Or perhaps you simply want to tour all the highlights as quickly and as comfortably as possible? Then a minibus with expert commentary is what you need. And what about a balloon ride or an electric Segway tour? The choice is yours!

🏙🚢 Bruges by boat

A visit to Bruges isn't complete without a boat trip on its canals. Go aboard at any of the five landing stages (consult city map) for a half-hour trip that allows you to appreciate the most noteworthy delights of the city from a completely different angle.

OPEN > March to mid-November: daily, 10.00 a.m.-6.00 p.m., last departure at 5.30 p.m.

PRICE > € 8.00; children aged 4 to 11 (accompanied by an adult): € 4.00; children under 4: free; Brugge City Card (during the period 1/3 to 14/11): free

🏙🚢 Lamme Goedzak (steam wheeler) Damme

The nostalgic river boat 'Lamme Goedzak', with room for 170 passengers, sails back and forth between Bruges and the centre of Damme, the town of the local folk hero Tijl Uilenspiegel (Owlglass), whose friend was called ... Lamme Goedzak!

OPEN > During the period 1/4 to 30/9: departures from Bruges to Damme, daily at 10.00 a.m., 12.00 p.m., 2.00 p.m. and 4.00 p.m.; departures from Damme to Bruges, daily at 11.00 a.m., 1.00 p.m., 3.00 p.m. and 5.00 p.m.

PRICE > € 8.00 (one-way ticket) or € 11.00 (return ticket); 65+: € 7.50 (one-way ticket) or € 10.00 (return ticket); children aged 3 to 11: € 6.50 (one-way ticket) or € 9.00 (return ticket); Brugge City Card: € 8.00 (return ticket)

MEETING POINT > Embark in Bruges at the Noorweegse Kaai 31 (City map: J1)

INFO > Tel. +32 (0)50 28 86 10, www.boot damme-brugge.be; public transport:

scheduled bus no. 4, bus stop: Sasplein near the Dampoort; from there it is a 5-10 minute walk to the landing stage in Bruges

🚢 Port Cruise Zeebrugge

The port cruise departs from the old fishing port on board of the *Zephira*, a passenger ship. The tour takes in the naval base, the Pierre Vandamme Lock (one of the largest locks in the world), the gas terminal, the wind turbine park, the 'tern' island, the cruise ships and the dredging vessels. You will also see how the massive container ships are unloaded at the quay. Each visitor is given an easy-to-use audio-visual guide in the desired language. You can also download the information on your smart phone. An experience that offers a unique insight into the port and its manifold activities.

OPEN > During the period 1/4 to 15/10: weekends and public holidays at 2.00 p.m.; during the period 1/7 to 31/8, daily at 2.00 p.m. and 4.00 p.m; during the period 1/8 to 17/8: daily extra round trip at 11.00 a.m.

PRICE > € 9.50; 60+ and students: € 9.00; children aged 3 to 11: € 7.00; Brugge City Card: € 7.00. Tickets are purchased on board.

MEETING POINT > Embark at the landing stage at the end of the Tijdokstraat (old fishing port), Zeebrugge

INFO > Tel. +32 (0)59 70 62 94 (for extra departures outside the fixed sailing times), www.franlis.be; public transport: train Bruges-Zeebrugge, from the station Zeebrugge-Dorp: about 15 to 20 minutes on foot or from the station Zeebrugge-Strand: coast tram (direction: Knokke), to tram stop: Zeebrugge-Kerk (church) and then a 5 minute walk

Bruges on foot

Are you not tired from all that walking? Do you still want to discover more of the many different facets and important sights of Bruges? If so, hurry along to the 🛈 tourist office on 't Zand (Concertgebouw) or at the Markt (Historium). Here, you can register for a fascinating two-hour walk in the expert company of an officially certified guide.

OPEN > January/February/March/November/December 🏛️: Monday, Wednesday and Saturday at 4.00 p.m. and Sunday at 10.30 a.m.

During the Easter holidays (26/3 to 10/4): Monday to Saturday at 2.30 p.m. and Sunday at 10.30 a.m.

April/May/June/September/October: Saturday at 2.30 p.m. and Sunday at 10.30 a.m.

July/August: Monday to Saturday at 2.30 p.m. and Sunday at 10.30 a.m.

On 27/3 (Easter), 28/3 (Easter Monday), 15/5 (Whit Sunday), 21/7 (national holiday), 15/8 (Assumption of Mary) and 25/12 (Christmas) at 10.30 a.m. On 6/5 (Ascension Friday) at 2.30 p.m. On 5/5 (Ascension Day) there will be no walk.

PRICE > € 12.50; children under 12: free; Brugge City Card (during the period 1/11 to 31/3): free

MEETING POINT > The walk starts at the 🛈 tourist office 't Zand (Concertgebouw)

LANGUAGES > English, Dutch, French

TICKETS > 🛈 Tourist office at the Markt (Historium) and 't Zand (Concertgebouw) or www.ticketsbrugge.be

---

TIP

Download the Xplore Bruges app (available for iOS and Android), the new media platform of the City of Bruges that shows you the way for various thematic and interactive walking and cycling routes. What's more, if you download the selected route(s) in advance, it is possible to use the app offline.

Photo Tour Brugge

Whether you are a photography expert or a photography novice, during the Photo Tour Andy McSweeney will take you to all the most photogenic spots in town! What are the 'must-have' shots for the photo reportage of your city trip to Bruges? You will learn this and lots more beside during a fascinating two-hour walk, complete with dozens of practical photography tips from Andy.

(Read more about Andy McSweeney in the interview on page 128-131.)

OPEN > Four walks are organized each day, each with a different theme: 'Edges of Brugge' (10.00 a.m.) focuses on the side streets and canals; 'Essential Brugge' (1.00 p.m.) zooms in on the toppers; during 'Hidden Brugge' (4.00 p.m.) you will go in search of some of the city's less well known corners; the private tour 'Shades of Brugge' (7.00 p.m.) allows you to experience the evening delights of the city.

PRICE > Themed tours: € 50.00; every paying participant receives five Bruges photos, specially taken by Andy McSweeney; every participating photographer can bring along one other non-photographer free of charge. Maximum of 5 photographers per walk. Private tour: € 200.00 (max. 3 photographing participants). Reservation is required, but is possible on the day, subject to availability.

MEETING POINT > Basilica of the Holy Blood, on the Burg
LANGUAGES > English, but also Dutch and/or French on request
INFO > Tel. +32 (0)486 17 52 75, www.phototourbrugge.com

Running around Bruges

Tourist Run Brugge – guided tours
Accompanied by a guide you run – at a gentle pace – through the streets and alleyways of Bruges. Because you either run early in the morning or early in the evening, you can freely admire Bruges. The circuit is 9.5 km long. With the explanation that you receive along the way, you should allow 1 to 1.5 hours for completion.

OPEN > Monday, Tuesday, Thursday and Friday at 5.00 p.m., 6.00 p.m., 7.00 p.m. or 8.00 p.m.; Wednesday, Saturday and Sunday at 7.00 a.m., 8.00 a.m., 9.00 a.m., 5.00 p.m., 6.00 p.m., 7.00 p.m., 8.00 p.m. or 9.00 p.m. Reservation is required.

PRICE > € 30.00 per person; for 2 runners: € 25.00 per person; for 3 runners: € 20.00 per person

MEETING POINT > At the statue of Jan Breydel and Pieter de Coninck on the Markt. If requested in advance, you can be picked up from wherever you are staying (hotel, etc.). The run also ends on the Markt.

INFO > Tel. +32 (0)473 88 37 17, www.touristrunbrugge.be

🐎 Bruges by horse-drawn carriage

The carriage ride along Bruges' historic winding streets takes thirty minutes. Halfway through the ride the carriage briefly stops at the Beguinage. The coachman gives expert commentary en route.

OPEN > Daily, 9.00 a.m.-6.00 p.m.; July and August, 9.00 a.m.-10.00 p.m.

PRICE > € 50.00 per carriage; a carriage seats up to 5 people

MEETING POINT > Markt, but at the Burg on Wednesday morning (market day)

INFO > www.hippo.be/koets

🚌 Bruges by bus

🚌 City Tour Bruges

The mini buses of City Tour provide a guided tour that passes all the most beautiful spots in the city. Every half hour, they depart for a 50 minute drive along the most important highlights of the town.

OPEN > Daily, every half hour (also on Sundays and public holidays). The first bus leaves at 10.00 a.m. During the period 1/1 to 31/1, the last bus leaves at 3.30 p.m.; during the periods 1/2 to 15/2 and 1/11 to 31/12 at 4.00 p.m.; during the period 16/2 to 15/3 at 5.00 p.m.; during the periods 16/3 to 30/4 and 1/10 to 15/10 at 6.00 p.m.; during the period 1/5 to 30/9 at 7.00 p.m. and during the period 16/10 to 31/10 at 4.30 p.m. There are no departures at 1.30 p.m. and 6.30 p.m.

PRICE > € 20.00 per person; children aged 6 to 11 years: € 15.00; children under 6: free; Brugge City Card (during the period 1/1 to 29/2 and 15/11 to 28/2/2017): free

MEETING POINT > Markt

LANGUAGES > Individual headphones provide explanations in one of 16 available languages.

INFO > Tel. +32 (0)50 35 50 24 (Monday to Friday, 10.00 a.m-12.00 p.m.), www.citytour.be

Bruges by bike

QuasiMundo Biketours:
Bruges by bike
Riding through the narrow streets, you
will discover the charming character of
medieval Bruges. The fascinating stories of the guide will catapult you back
in time to the era when knights and
counts ruled over the city. On the way,
of course, you will stop to enjoy a
thirst-quenching Belgian beer.
OPEN > During the period 1/3 to 15/11:
daily, 10.00 a.m.-12.30 p.m. Reservation
is required.
PRICE > Including bike, guide, raincoat
and drink in a local bar: € 28.00; youngsters aged 9 to 26 and students: € 26.00.
If you bring your own bike, then the rates
are as follows: adults: € 16.00; youngsters (aged 9 to 26) and students:
€ 15.00. Children under 8: free

MEETING POINT > At the town hall on the
Burg, 10 minutes before departure
LANGUAGES > English, other languages
on request
INFO > Tel. +32 (0)50 33 07 75 or +32
(0)478 28 15 21, www.quasimundo.eu
*(see also 'Excursions leaving from
Bruges', page 155-156)*

Bruges on a Segway

Moment
If you want to discover Bruges in an
original manner, why not choose a Segway tour? A Segway is a self-stabilising
electric vehicle with two wheels that
you operate while standing on it in an
upright position. In addition to the city
tour, which takes you to the historic
sites and the most magnificent monuments and buildings in Bruges, you can
also opt for the chocolate tour, the

brewery tour (with a visit to the Halve Maan Brewery) or an evening tour in which you combine a ride through the beautifully illuminated inner city with a three-course menu.

OPEN > Guided tour on Monday at 12.00 p.m., 2.00 p.m. and 4.00 p.m.; on Tuesday, Thursday and Friday at 10.00 a.m., 12.00 p.m., 2.00 p.m. and 4.00 p.m. (on Saturday also at 6.00 p.m., if there are at least 4 participants); on Sunday at 10.00 a.m., 12.00 p.m. and 2.00 p.m. Reservation is required, but can be made on the day, subject to availability. At least 2 persons per tour

ADDITIONAL CLOSING DAYS > 1/1, 19/1 to 18/2, 18/7 to 25/7 and 25/12

PRICE > Guide included: € 35.00 (1 hour) or € 50.00 (2 hours)

MEETING POINT > Sint-Jakobsstraat 44

LANGUAGES > English, Dutch, French, German

INFO > Tel. +32 (0)50 68 87 70 or +32 (0)495 90 60 60, www.segwaybrugge.be

Bruges by hot air balloon

🎫 Bruges Ballooning

The most adventurous and probably the most romantic way to discover Bruges is by hot-air balloon. Bruges Ballooning organizes both a morning flight (including a champagne breakfast) and an evening flight (including a bite to eat, champagne or a beer) over Bruges. The whole trip lasts for three hours, with at least one hour in the air.

OPEN > During the period 1/4 to 31/10: daily flights, but only if booked in advance; bookings can be made on the day itself with a few hours' notice, providing there are no prior reservations.

PRICE > € 180.00; children aged 4 to 12: € 110.00; Brugge City Card: € 135.00

MEETING POINT > You will be picked up and dropped off wherever you are staying.

INFO > Tel. +32 (0)475 97 28 87, www.bruges-ballooning.com

Museums, places of interest and attractions

Some places are so special, so breathtaking or so unique that you simply have to see them. Bruges is filled to the brim with wonderful witnesses of a prosperous past. Although the Flemish primitives are undoubtedly Bruges' showpiece attraction, museum devotees in search of much more will not be disappointed. Indeed, the Bruges range of attractions is truly magnificent. From modern plastic art by way of Michelangelo's world-famous *Madonna and Child* to the brand new Lace Centre. It's all there for you to discover! With the Brugge City Card, you can visit numerous museums, places of interest and attractions for free 🎫 or with a good discount 🎫.

🏙️ 01 08 ⛪ Adornesdomein – Jeruzalemkapel (Adornes Estate – Jerusalem Chapel)

The Adornes domain consists of the 15th-century Jerusalem Chapel (a jewel of medieval architecture built by this rich merchant family), the Adornes mansion and a series of adjacent almshouses. In the new multimedia museum, you can follow in the footsteps of Anselm Adornes and learn all about the world in which he lived. You will go on a pilgrimage, take part in a joust and meet many notable persons of the time, such as the King of Scotland, the Lords of Gruuthuse and the Dukes of Burgundy.

OPEN > Monday to Saturday, 10.00 a.m.-5.00 p.m.
ADDITIONAL CLOSING DATES >
All (Belgian) public holidays
PRICE > € 7.00; 65+: € 5.00; youngsters aged 7 to 25: € 3.50; children under 7: free; Brugge City Card: free
INFO > Peperstraat 3A, tel. +32 (0)50 33 88 83, www.adornes.org

🏙️ 02 Archeologiemuseum (Archaeological Museum)

This museum presents the unwritten history of Bruges. Its motto: feel your past beneath your feet. Discover the history of the city through different kinds of search and hands-on activities. A fascinating mix of archaeological finds, riddles, replicas and reconstructions shed light on daily life in times gone by, from the home to the workplace and from birth till death.

OPEN > Tuesday to Sunday, 9.30 a.m.-12.30 p.m. and 1.30 p.m.-5.00 p.m.; last admission: 12.00 p.m. and 4.30 p.m. (open on Easter Monday and Whit Monday)
ADDITIONAL CLOSING DATES >
1/1, 5/5 (1.00 p.m.-5.00 p.m.) and 25/12
PRICE > € 4.00; 65+ and youngsters aged 12 to 25: € 3.00; children under 12: free; Brugge City Card: free
INFO > Mariastraat 36A, tel. +32 (0)50 44 87 43, www.museabrugge.be

🏙️ 03 Arentshuis

In this elegant 18th-century town house with its picturesque garden, the work of the versatile British artist Frank Brangwyn (1867-1956) is on display on the top

floor. Brangwyn was both a graphic artist and a painter, as well as a designer of carpets, furniture and ceramics. The ground floor is the setting for temporary plastic art exhibitions.

OPEN > Tuesday to Sunday, 9.30 a.m.-5.00 p.m.; last admission: 4.30 p.m. (open on Easter Monday and Whit Monday)

ADDITIONAL CLOSING DATES > 1/1, 5/5 (1.00 p.m.-5.00 p.m.) and 25/12

PRICE > € 4.00; 65+ and youngsters aged 12 to 25: € 3.00; children under 12: free; Brugge City Card: free; combination ticket with Groeninge Museum possible *(see pages 84-85)*

INFO > Dijver 16, tel. +32 (0)50 44 87 43, www.museabrugge.be

⬛🏳 ♿ 01 Basiliek van het Heilig Bloed (Basilica of the Holy Blood)

The double church, dedicated to Our Lady and Saint Basil in the 12th century and a basilica since 1923, consists of a lower church that has maintained its Romanesque character and a neo-Gothic upper church, in which the relic of the Holy Blood is preserved.

The treasury, with numerous valuable works of art, is also worth a visit.

OPEN > Monday to Saturday: 9.30 a.m.-12.00 p.m. and 2.00 p.m.-5.00 p.m.; Sunday: 9.30 a.m.-11.00 a.m. and 2.00 p.m.-5.00 p.m.; during the period 15/11 to 31/3 closed on Wednesday afternoon

PRICE > Double church: free; treasury: € 2.50; children under 13: free; Brugge City Card: free

INFO > Burg 13, tel. +32 (0)50 33 67 92, www.holyblood.com

⬛🏳 ♿ 02 02 04 Begijnhof (Beguinage)

The 'Princely Beguinage Ten Wijn-gaarde' with its white-coloured house fronts, tranquil convent garden and beguinage museum was founded in 1245. This little piece of world heritage was once the home of the beguines, emancipated lay-women who nevertheless led a pious and celibate life. Nowadays, the Beguinage is inhabited by the Sisters of the Order of Saint Benedict. In the small beguine house, you can still gain insights into what daily life was like in the 17th century. Please note: the entrance gates are always closed (and remain closed) at 6.30 p.m.

OPEN > Beguinage: daily, 6.30 a.m.-6.30 p.m.; Beguine's house: Monday to Saturday, 10.00 a.m.-5.00 p.m., Sunday 2.30 p.m.-5.00 p.m.

PRICE > Beguinage: free; Beguine's house: € 2.00; 65+: € 1.50; children aged 8 to 11 and students (on display of a valid student card): € 1.00; Brugge City Card: free

INFO > Begijnhof 24-28-30, tel. +32 (0)50
33 00 11, www.monasteria.org,
www.bezinningshuizen.be

🏛 ❤ 05 10 Belfort (Belfry)

The most important of Bruges' towers
stands 83 metres tall. It houses,
amongst other things, a carillon with
47 melodious bells. In the reception
area, (waiting) visitors can discover all
kinds of interesting information about
the history and working of this unique
world-heritage protected belfry. Those
who take on the challenge of climbing
the tower can pause for a breather on
the way up in the old treasury, where
the city's charters, seal and public
funds were kept during the Middle
Ages, and also at the level of the impressive clock or in the carillonneur's
chamber. Finally, after a tiring
366 steps, your efforts will be rewarded with a breath-taking and unforgettable panoramic view of Bruges and
her surroundings.
OPEN > Daily, 9.30 a.m.-6.00 p.m.; last
admission: 5.00 p.m. For safety reasons,
only a limited number of persons will be
allowed to visit the tower at the same
time. Reservations are not possible.

Each visitor has to wait in line. Please
consider a certain waiting period.
ADDITIONAL CLOSING DATES >
1/1, 5/5 (1.00 p.m.-6.00 p.m.) and 25/12
PRICE > € 10.00; 65+ and youngsters
aged 6 to 25: € 8.00; children under 6:
free; Brugge City Card: free
INFO > Markt 7, tel. +32 (0)50 44 87 43,
www.museabrugge.be

Bezoekerscentrum Lissewege – Heiligenmuseum (Visitors Centre Lissewege – Saints' Museum)

The Visitors Centre tells the story of
'the white village', which dates back
through more than a thousand years of
history. Unique photographs, maps,
models, paintings and a collection of
archaeological discoveries all illus-
trate this glorious past. In the Saints'
Museum, you can admire an equally

unique collection of more than 130 antique statues of patron saints.

OPEN > During the Easter holidays (26/3 to 10/4), during Pentecost and Ascension weekends, during the period 15/6 to 15/9 and on 17/9, 18/9, 24/9 and 25/9: daily, 2.00 p.m.-5.30 p.m.

PRICE > Saints' Museum: € 2.00; museum + coffee/tea: € 3.50; children under 12: € 1.00

INFO > Oude Pastoriestraat 5, Lissewege, tel. +32 (0)50 55 29 55, www.lissewege.be; public transport: train Brugge-Zeebrugge

Boudewijn Seapark Bruges

Welcome to the Boudewijn Seapark, where dolphins steal the show with their spectacular leaps and where sea lions and seals perform the craziest tricks. But it is not only the sea mammals in this family park that will charm you, but also the 20 outdoor park attractions that offer guaranteed fun for young and old alike. Finally, *Bobo's Indoor* has 12 great indoor attractions, as well as *Bobo's Aqua Splash*, providing 1,100 square meters of wonderful water fun.

OPEN > During the period 26/3 to 6/11. During the Easter holidays (26/3 to 10/4) and weekends in April: 10.00 a.m.-5.00 p.m.; in May and June: daily, except on Wednesday, 10.00 a.m.-5.00 p.m.; in July and August: daily, 10.00 a.m.-6.00 p.m.; in September: Saturday and Sunday, 10.00 a.m.-6.00 p.m.; during the autumn holidays (29/10 to 6/11): 10.00 a.m.-5.00 p.m. Please consult the website to see which attractions are open.

ADDITIONAL CLOSING DATES > 1/1, 24/12, 25/12 and 31/12

PRICE > All-in ticket: € 25.50; 65+ and children taller than 1 metre and under 12 years old: € 21.50; children between 85 cm and 99 cm: € 9.00; Brugge City Card: € 16.50

INFO > A. De Baeckestraat 12, Sint-Michiels, tel. +32 (0)50 38 38 38, www.boudewijnseapark.be. Tickets at the amusement park entrance or at the 🛈 tourist office 't Zand (Concertgebouw). Boudewijn Sea Park is situated just outside the city centre and is connected to the Bicycle Route Network; public transport: scheduled bus no. 7 or no. 17, bus stop: Boudewijnpark

🚻 ⑫ Brouwerij De Halve Maan (Brewery)

The Halve Maan (Half Moon) is an authentic and historic brewery in the centre of Bruges. This 'home' brewery is a family business with a tradition stretching back through six generations to 1856. This is where the Bruges city beer – the *Brugse Zot* – is brewed: a strong-tasting, high-fermentation beer based on malt, hops and special yeast. There are guided tours of the brewery every day in a number of different languages. After the tour, visitors are treated to the blond version of the *Brugse Zot*. If you want to take a souvenir back home with you, why not pay a visit to the museum shop?

OPEN > Daily, 11.00 a.m.-4.00 p.m. (on Saturday until 5.00 p.m.); there is a tour every hour with a Dutch, French and English-speaking guide. German-speaking guide on request

ADDITIONAL CLOSING DATES > 1/1, 11/1 to 15/1, 18/1 to 22/1, 25/1 to 29/1, 24/12 and 25/12

PRICE > Including refreshment: € 8.50; children aged 6 to 12: € 4.50; children under 6: free; Brugge City Card: free

INFO > Walplein 26, tel. +32 (0)50 44 42 22, www.halvemaan.be

⑭ Brugs Biermuseum (Bruges Beer Museum)

The Bruges Beer Museum has been opened on the upper floors of the historic post office on the Market Square. With a mini iPad as your guide, you will discover all the most fascinating features of beer (and that includes tasting!). Immerse yourself in the beer history of Belgium and of Bruges. Discover the many different types of beer and unravel the mysteries of the brewery process. The kids' tour tells the story of 'The bear of Bruges'.

OPEN > Daily, 10.00 a.m.-6.30 p.m.; last admission at 5.00 p.m.

ADDITIONAL CLOSING DATES > 1/1 and 25/12

PRICE > Including iPad (with headphones) and 3 beer samples: € 14.00; including iPad (with headphones) but without beer samples: € 9.00; children aged 5 to 15 (kids tour): € 6.00; children under 5: free; Family Pass (2 adults and max. 3 children): € 32.00 with beer tasting or € 22.00 without tasting

INFO > Breidelstraat 3 (Post Office), tel. +32 (0)479 35 95 67, www.brugesbeermuseum.com

🏙 `01` `03` `08` `15` Brugse Vrije (Liberty of Bruges)

From this mansion, erected between 1722 and 1727, Bruges' rural surroundings were governed. The building functioned as a court of justice between 1795 and 1984. Today the city archives are stored here. They safeguard Bruges' written memory. The premises also boast an old assize court and a renaissance hall with a monumental 16th-century timber, marble and alabaster fireplace made by Lanceloot Blondeel.

OPEN > Daily, 9.30 a.m.-12.30 p.m. and 1.30 p.m.-5.00 p.m.; last admission: 12.00 p.m. and 4.30 p.m.

ADDITIONAL CLOSING DATES > 1/1, 5/5 (1.00 p.m.-5.00 p.m.) and 25/12

PRICE > Including City Hall visit: € 4.00; 65+ and youngsters aged 12 to 25: € 3.00; children under 12: free; Brugge City Card: free. Tickets are sold in the town hall.

INFO > Burg 11A, tel. +32 (0)50 44 87 43, www.museabrugge.be

🏙 `16` Choco-Story (Chocolate Museum)

The museum dips its visitors in the history of cocoa and chocolate. From the Maya and the Spanish conquistadores to the chocolate connoisseurs of today. A chocolate hunt gives children the chance to discover the museum. Chocolates are made by hand and sampled on the premises. In 2015, the museum opened a thematic Choco-Jungle bar at Vlamingstraat 31, just a 5-minute walk away.

OPEN > During the period 1/9 to 30/6: daily, 10.00 a.m.-5.00 p.m.; last admission: 4.15 p.m.; during the period 1/7 to 31/8: daily, 10.00 a.m.-6.00 p.m.; last admission: 5.15 p.m.

ADDITIONAL CLOSING DATES > 1/1, 11/1 to 15/1, 24/12, 25/12 and 31/12

PRICE > € 8.00; 65+ and students: € 7.00; children aged 6 to 11: € 5.00; children under 6: free; Brugge City Card: free; several combination tickets possible *(see page 93)*

INFO > Wijnzakstraat 2, tel. +32 (0)50 61 22 37, www.choco-story.be

🏙 ♿ `17` Concertgebouw - Open Huis (Concert Hall - Open House)

From September 2016 onwards, you will be able to visit the Concert Hall, a jewel of contemporary architecture that houses a fascinating collection of modern art. The brand new visitor tour will show you

why this artistic temple is so popular with the public and performers alike. You will also play music yourself during a playful stop in the Sound Factory, an interactive space for sound art.

OPEN > From September 2016 onwards: Wednesday to Saturday, 2.00 p.m.-6.00 p.m., last admission at 5.30 p.m.; Sunday, 10.00 a.m.-12.30 p.m., last entrance at 12.00 p.m.

ADDITIONAL CLOSING DATES > 1/11, 11/11 and 25/12

PRICE > € 8.00; Brugge City Card: free

INFO > 't Zand 34, tel. +32 (0)50 47 69 99, www.concertgebouw.be

Cozmix volkssterrenwacht (Public Observatory) Beisbroek

In the Cozmix observatory you will be able to admire the beauty of the sun, moon and planets in glorious close-up, thanks to the powerful telescope. In the planetarium more than 7,000 stars are projected onto the interior of the dome. Spectacular video images take you on a journey through the mysteries of the universe: you will fly over the surface of Mars and pass through the rings of Saturn. The artistic planet-pathway (with sculptures by Jef Claerhout) will complete your voyage of discovery into outer space.

OPEN > Wednesday and Sunday, 2.30 p.m.-6.00 p.m., Friday, 8.00 p.m.-10.00 p.m.; planetarium shows on Wednesday and Sunday at 3.00 p.m. and 4.30 p.m., on Friday at 8.30 p.m. During (Belgian) school holidays there are extra shows on Monday, Tuesday and Thursday at 3.00 p.m. Presentations in a foreign language are given on Wednesday at 4.30 p.m.: the first, third (and fifth) week of the month in French; the second and fourth week in English.

ADDITIONAL CLOSING DATES > 1/1 and 25/12

PRICE > € 5.00; youngsters aged 5 to 17: € 4.00

INFO > Zeeweg 96, Sint-Andries, tel. +32 (0)50 39 05 66, www.cozmix.be; public transport: scheduled bus no. 52, no. 53 or no. 55, bus stop: Varsenare Zeeweg. An approximate 20-minute walk from the bus stop.

18 Museum-Gallery Xpo Salvador Dalí

In the Cloth Halls, you can admire a fantastic collection of world-famous

graphics and statues by the great artist Dalí. They are all authentic works of art that are described in the Catalogues Raisonnés, which details Salvador Dalí's oeuvre. The collection is presented in a sensational Daliesque décor of mirrors, gold and shocking pink.

OPEN > Daily, 10.00 a.m.-6.00 p.m.

ADDITIONAL CLOSING DATES >
1/1 and 25/12

PRICE > € 10.00; 65+ and students:
€ 8.00; children under 12: free; Brugge City Card: free

INFO > Markt 7, tel. +32 (0)50 33 83 44, www.dali-interart.be

🏙 21 Diamantmuseum Brugge (Bruges Diamond Museum)

Did you know that the technique of cutting diamonds was first applied in Bruges almost 550 years ago? The Bruges Diamond Museum tells this story in a series of fascinating exhibition displays. And there is a live demonstration of diamond cutting each day – a memorable experience, not to be missed! In the diamond laboratory, microscopes and other equipment allow visitors, both young and old alike, to discover

the true beauty of diamonds in all their many facets.

OPEN > Daily, 10.30 a.m.-5.30 p.m. Demonstrations: daily, at 12.15 p.m.; during the weekends, (Belgian) school holidays and the period 1/4 to 31/10: extra demonstration at 3.15 p.m. (visitors need to be present 15 minutes in advance)

ADDITIONAL CLOSING DATES >
1/1, 11/1 to 22/1 and 25/12

PRICE > Museum: € 8.00, museum + diamond-cutting demo: € 11.00; 65+, students (on display of a valid student card) and children aged 6 to 12: museum: € 7.00, museum + diamond-cutting demo: € 10.00; children under 6: free; Brugge City Card: free; a combination ticket is possible *(see page 93)*

INFO > Katelijnestraat 43, tel. +32 (0)50 34 20 56, www.diamond museum.be

🏙 23 Foltermuseum De Oude Steen (Torture Museum)

The Oude Steen is one of the oldest prisons in Europe. The building has been renovated and transformed into a torture museum, with an extraordinary collection of artefacts and lifelike wax sculptures that shed a light on the con-

troversial use of torture, where it was once thought that the end – justice – justified the means.

OPEN > Daily, 10.30 a.m.-6.30 p.m.
ADDITIONAL CLOSING DATES > 1/1, 24/12 (3.00 p.m.-6.30 p.m.) and 25/12
PRICE > € 7.00; 60+ and students: € 5.00; children under 6: free; Brugge City Card: free
INFO > Wollestraat 29, tel. +32 (0)50 73 41 34, www.torturemuseum.be

08 24 Frietmuseum (Belgian Fries Museum)

This didactical museum sketches the history of the potato, Belgian fries and the various sauces and dressings that accompany this most delicious and most famous of Belgian comestibles. The museum is housed in the Saai-

halle, one of Bruges' most attractive buildings. Show your entrance ticket and enjoy a € 0.40 discount on a portion of French fries (in the basement).

OPEN > Daily, 10.00 a.m.-5.00 p.m.; last admission: 4.15 p.m.
ADDITIONAL CLOSING DATES > 1/1, 11/1 to 15/1, 24/12, 25/12 and 31/12
PRICE > € 7.00; 65+ and students: € 6.00; children aged 6 to 11: € 5.00; children under 6: free; Brugge City Card: free; several combination tickets possible *(see page 93)*
INFO > Vlamingstraat 33, tel. +32 (0)50 34 01 50, www.frietmuseum.be

07 25 Gentpoort (Gate of Ghent)

The Gate of Ghent is one of four remaining medieval city gates. An entrance for foreigners, a border with the outside world for the townspeople of Bruges. The gate was a part of the city's defences as well as a passageway for the movement of produce and merchandise. Note the statue in the niche above the roadway: this is Saint Adrian, who was believed to protect the city during times of plague. The Ghent Gate

is at its most beautiful in the evening, when it is quite literally in the spotlight.
OPEN > Saturday and Sunday, 9.30 a.m.-12.30 p.m. and 1.30 p.m.-5.00 p.m.; last admission: 12.00 p.m. and 4.30 p.m.
ADDITIONAL CLOSING DATE > 25/12
PRICE > € 4.00; 65+ and youngsters aged 12 to 25: € 3.00; children under 12: free; Brugge City Card: free
INFO > Gentpoortvest, tel. +32 (0)50 44 87 43, www.museabrugge.be

26 Gezellemuseum (Gezelle Museum)

This literary and biographical museum about the life of Guido Gezelle (1830-1899), one of Flanders' most famous poets, was established in the house where he was born, situated in a peaceful working-class district of the city. In addition to displays about his life and works, there are also temporary presentations about (literary) art. Next to the house there is a romantic garden, with Jan Fabre's *The Man Who Gives a Light* as the main attraction.
OPEN > Tuesday to Sunday: 9.30 a.m.-12.30 p.m. and 1.30 p.m.-5.00 p.m.; last admission: 12.00 a.m. and

4.30 p.m. (open on Easter Monday and Whit Monday)
ADDITIONAL CLOSING DATES > 1/1, 5/5 (1.00 p.m.-5.00 p.m.) and 25/12
PRICE > € 4.00; 65+ and youngsters aged 12 to 25: € 3.00; children under 12: free; Brugge City Card: free
INFO > Rolweg 64, tel. +32 (0)50 44 87 43, www.museabrugge.be

27 Groeningemuseum (Groeninge Museum)

The Groeninge Museum provides a varied overview of the history of Belgian visual art, with the world-renowned Flemish primitives as a highlight. In this museum you can see, amongst other masterpieces, *The Virgin and Child with Canon Van der Paele* by Jan van Eyck and the *Moreel Triptych* by Hans Memling. You will also marvel at the top 18th and 19th-century neoclassical pieces, masterpieces of Flemish Expressionism and post-war modern art.
OPEN > Tuesday to Sunday: 9.30 a.m.-5.00 p.m.; last admission: 4.30 p.m. (open on Easter Monday and Whit Monday)
ADDITIONAL CLOSING DATES > 1/1, 5/5 (1.00 p.m.-5.00 p.m.) and 25/12

PRICE > Including Arentshuis: € 8.00;
65+ and youngsters aged 12 to 25:
€ 6.00; children under 12: free; Brugge
City Card: free; a combination ticket is
possible *(see page 93)*
INFO > Dijver 12, tel. +32 (0)50 44 87 43,
www.museabrugge.be

28 Gruuthusemuseum (Gruuthuse Museum)

The luxurious city palace of the lords
of Gruuthuse is closed until 2018 for
extensive restoration work.
INFO > Dijver 17, tel. +32 (0)50 44 87 43,
www.museabrugge.be

🎫 ℹ️ ⊠ 📷 🚌 ♿ 29

Historium Bruges

Relive the Golden Age of Bruges. Using
film and special effects, seven themed
rooms will take you back in time, to a
day in 1435. Thrill to the romantic tale of
Jacob, an apprentice of Jan Van Eyck,
and discover the interactive exhibition
space, complete with touchscreens.
Enjoy the panoramic view over the
Market and finish with a glass of something pleasant in the Duvelorium Grand
Beer Café.

OPEN > Daily, 10.00 a.m.-6.00 p.m.,
last admission: 5.00 p.m.
ADDITIONAL CLOSING DATE > 1/1
PRICE > Including audio-guide (available in 10 languages): € 13.50; students
(on display of a valid student card):
€ 10.00; children aged 3 to 14: € 7.50;
including tasting (3 beers of 16 cl) in
Duvelorium: € 20.50; Family Pass
(2 adults and max. 3 children): € 37.00;
Brugge City Card: free; a combination
ticket is possible *(see page 93)*
INFO > Markt 1, tel. +32 (0)50 27 03 11,
www.historium.be

09 Hof Bladelin (Bladelin Court)

In around 1440, Pieter Bladelin, treasur-
er of the Order of the Golden Fleece,
commissioned the construction of
Bladelin Court. In the 15th century
the powerful Florentine banking family
of de' Medici set up a branch here.
The stone medallion portraits of Lorenzo de' Medici and his wife still grace the
picturesque inner court, which was recently restored to its former glory.
OPEN > Inner court, rooms and chapel:
Monday to Friday, 10.00 a.m.-12.00 p.m.

and 2.00 p.m.-5.00 p.m.; visits are only possible with a guide and by appointment.

ADDITIONAL CLOSING DATES > All (Belgian) public holidays
PRICE > Inner court, rooms and chapel: € 5.00 (price guide not included); garden: € 1.00
INFO > Naaldenstraat 19, tel. +32 (0)50 33 64 34

🛗 ♿ 31 Kantcentrum (Lace Centre)

Since 2014, the Lace Centre has been housed in the renovated old lace school of the Sisters of the Immaculate Conception. The story of Bruges lace is told in the lace museum on the ground floor. Multimedia installations and testimonies from international lace experts help to explain the various different types of lace and their geographical origin, as well as focusing on the lace industry and lace education in Bruges. In an interactive way, using touch screens, the visitor is introduced to the complexities of the 'spellenwerk': the making of lace with pins and bobbins. Demonstrations and various courses are organized in the lace workshop on the first floor. *(Also read the interview with Kumiko Nakazaki on pages 120-123.)*

OPEN > Daily, 9.30 a.m.-5.00 p.m.; last admission: 4.30 p.m.; demonstrations: Monday to Saturday, 2.00 p.m.-5.00 p.m. (except Belgian public holidays)
ADDITIONAL CLOSING DATES > Museum: 1/1, 5/5 and 25/12
PRICE > € 5.00; 65+ and youngsters aged 12 to 25: € 4.00; children under 12: free; Brugge City Card: free; a combination ticket is possible *(see page 93)*
INFO > Balstraat 16, tel. +32 (0)50 33 00 72, www.kantcentrum.eu

🛗 33 Lumina Domestica (Lamp Museum)

The museum contains the world's largest collection of lamps and lights. More than 6.000 antiques tell the complete story of interior lighting, from the torch and paraffin lamp to the light bulb and LED. The small detour into the world of luminous animals and plants is particularly interesting. In this way you can discover, for example, the light mysteries of the glow-worm, the lantern fish and the small Chinese lantern.

OPEN > During the period 1/9 to 30/6: daily, 10.00 a.m.-5.00 p.m., last admission: 4.15 p.m.; during the period 1/7 to 31/8: daily, 10.00 a.m.-6.00 p.m., last admission: 5.15 p.m.

ADDITIONAL CLOSING DATES > 1/1, 11/1 to 15/1, 24/12, 25/12 and 31/12

PRICE > € 7.00; 65+ and students: € 6.00; children aged 6 to 11: € 5.00; children under 6: free; Brugge City Card: free; several combination tickets possible *(see page 93)*

INFO > Wijnzakstraat 2, tel. +32 (0)50 61 22 37, www.luminadomestica.be

Onze-Lieve-Vrouwekerk (Church of Our Lady)

The 115.5 metres high brick tower of the Church of Our Lady is a perfect illustration of the craftsmanship of Bruges' artisans. The church displays a valuable art collection: Michelangelo's world-famous Madonna and Child, countless paintings, 13th-century painted sepulch-

ers and the tombs of Mary of Burgundy and Charles the Bold. The choir was renovated in 2015 and the remarkable church interior can now once again be admired in all its splendour.

OPEN > Monday to Saturday, 9.30 a.m.-5.00 p.m.; Sunday and Holy Days, 1.30 p.m.-5.00 p.m.; last admission: 4.30 p.m., tickets for the museum section are on sale in the south transept. The church and the museum are not open to the public during nuptial and funeral masses. Useful to know: at the moment, large-scale renovation works are still being carried out, so the church is only partially accessible and many works of art cannot be viewed.

ADDITIONAL CLOSING DATES > Museum: 1/1, 5/5 and 25/12

PRICE > Church: free; museum: € 6.00; 65+ and youngsters aged 12 to 25: € 5.00; children under 12: free; Brugge City Card: free. There is a discount on the entrance price during the renovation.

INFO > Mariastraat, tel. +32 (0)50 44 87 43, www.museabrugge.be

Onze-Lieve-Vrouw-Bezoekingskerk Lissewege (Church of Our Lady of Visitation)

The brick Church of Our Lady of Visitation is a textbook example of 'coastal Gothic'. Its remarkable interior has a miraculous statue of the Virgin Mary (1625), an exceptional organ case and a beautifully sculptured rood loft and pulpit (1652). Anyone who makes the effort to climb all 264 steps of the squat, flat-topped tower will

be rewarded with a panoramic view over the polders towards Ostend and Bruges.

OPEN > Church: daily, 10.00 a.m.-5.00 p.m.; during the period 1/6 to 30/9, 9.00 a.m.-8.00 p.m. Tower: during the period 1/7 to 31/8, daily, 2.30 p.m.-5.30 p.m.
PRICE > Church: free. Tower: € 2.00; children under 12: € 0.50
INFO > Onder de Toren, Lissewege, tel. +32 (0)50 54 45 44 (church), +32 (0)487 49 92 14 (tower), www.lissewege.be; public transport: train Brugge-Zeebrugge

16 36 Onze-Lieve-Vrouw-ter-Potterie (Our Lady of the Pottery)

This hospital dates back to the 13th century, when nuns took on the care of pilgrims, travellers and the sick. In the 15th century, it evolved towards a more modern type of home for the elderly. The hospital wards with their valuable collection of works of art, monastic and religious relics and a range of objects used in nursing have been converted into a museum. The Gothic church with its baroque interior can also be visited.

OPEN > Tuesday to Sunday, 9.30 a.m.-12.30 p.m. and 1.30 p.m.-5.00 p.m.;

last admission: 12.00 p.m. and 4.30 p.m. (open on Easter Monday and Whit Monday)

ADDITIONAL CLOSING DATES > 1/1, 5/5 (1.00 p.m.-5.00 p.m.) and 25/12
PRICE > Church: free; museum: € 4.00; 65+ and youngsters aged 12 to 25: € 3.00; children under 12: free; Brugge City Card: free
INFO > Potterierei 79B, tel. +32 (0)50 44 87 43, www.museabrugge.be

17 Onze-Lieve-Vrouw-van-Blindekenskapel (Chapel of our Lady of the Blind)

The original wooden Chapel of Our Lady of Blindekens was erected in 1305 as an expression of gratitude to Our Lady after the Battle of Mons-en-Pévèle (1304). The current chapel dates from 1651. The mi-

raculous statue of Our Lady of Blindekens dates from the beginning of the 15th century. In order to fulfill the 'Bruges promise', which saw the men of the city returned safe home after the battle, the Blindekens procession has paraded through the streets of the city on 15th August every year since 1305. At the end of the parade, the women of Bruges offer a 36-pound candle in the Church of Our Lady of the Pottery.

OPEN > Daily, 9.00 a.m.-5.00 p.m.
PRICE > Free
INFO > Kreupelenstraat

🏙 05 38 Expo Picasso

The historic area of the former Hospital of Saint John (Old Saint John's) hosts a permanent exhibition of more than 300 original works of art by Pablo Picasso. Admire the engravings and rare illustrations as well as the drawings and ceramics of the world-famous artist. The exhibition outlines the evolution in his work: from his Spanish period to cubism to surrealism. A second exhibition shows some 100 works of art by Picasso's friend, Miró.

OPEN > Daily, 10.00 a.m.-5.00 p.m.

ADDITIONAL CLOSING DATES >
4/1 to 31/1 and 25/12
PRICE > € 10.00; 65+ and youngsters aged 7 to 18: € 8.00; children under 7: free; Brugge City Card: free
INFO > Site Oud Sint-Jan, Mariastraat 38, tel. +32 (0)50 47 61 08, www.expo-brugge.be

🏙 Seafront Zeebrugge

This maritime theme park, situated in the unique setting of the old fish market in Zeebrugge, allows you to explore the secrets of the Belgian fishing industry through the interactive exhibition 'Fish, from the boat right onto your plate' and discover the bustling world of the international port of Zeebrugge. The more restful visitors can enjoy the story of coastal tourism past and present, while the adventurous can play at being the master of the West-Hinder lightship or a sailor on an authentic Russian submarine. Children can enjoy themselves on the pirate island and in the ball pool. Also visit the large commemorative exhibition 'Besieged Coast, Occupied Port – Zeebrugge & WWI' about the First World War.

OPEN > During the period 1/9 to 30/6: daily, 10.00 a.m.-5.00 p.m.; during the period 1/7 to 31/8: daily, 10.00 a.m.-6.00 p.m; adapted opening hours in November and December: consult the website

ADDITIONAL CLOSING DATES >
1/1, 4/1 to 22/1 and 25/12

PRICE > Including visit to exhibitions: € 12.50; 60+ and students (on display of a valid student card): € 11.00; children under 12: € 9.00; children up to 1 metre (accompanied by an adult): free; Brugge City Card: € 8.50

INFO > Vismijnstraat 7, Zeebrugge, tel. +32 (0)50 55 14 15, www.seafront.be; public transport: train Brugge-Zeebrugge, from the station Zee-brugge-Dorp or Zeebrugge-Strand: coastal tram (direction: Knokke), stop: Zeebrugge-Kerk (Church)

2.00 p.m.-5.00 p.m., last admission both: 4.30 p.m. (both open on Easter Monday and Whit Monday)

ADDITIONAL CLOSING DATES >
1/1, 5/5 (1.00 p.m.-5.00 p.m.) and 25/12

PRICE > Including visit to the pharmacy: € 8.00; 65+ and youngsters aged 12 to 25: € 6.00; children under 12: free; Brugge City Card: free

INFO > Mariastraat 38, tel. +32 (0)50 44 87 43, www.museabrugge.be

39 Sint-Janshospitaal (Saint John's Hospital)

Saint John's Hospital has an eight hundred-year-old history of caring for pilgrims, travellers and the sick. Visit the medieval wards where the nuns and monks performed their work of mercy, as well as the chapel, and marvel at the impressive collection of archives, art works, medical instruments and six paintings by Hans Memling. Also worth a visit: the Diksmuide attic, the old dor-mitory, the adjoining custodian's room and the pharmacy.

OPEN > Museum: Tuesday to Sunday, 9.30 a.m.-5.00 p.m. Pharmacy: Tuesday to Sunday, 9.30 a.m.-11.45 a.m. and

40 Sint-Janshuismolen (Mill)
32 Koeleweimolen (Mill)

Windmills have graced Bruges' ram-parts ever since the construction of the outer city wall at the end of the 13th century. Today four specimens are left on Kruisvest. Sint-Janshuis Mill (1770) is still in its original spot and still grinding grain, just like its neigh-bour Koelewei Mill, which is being renovated and will therefore be closed until 2017.

OPEN > Sint-Janshuis Mill: during the period 1/4 to 30/9: Tuesday to Sunday, 9.30 a.m.-12.30 p.m. and 1.30 p.m.-5.00 p.m., last admission: 12.00 p.m.

and 4.30 p.m. (open on Whit Monday). Koelewei Mill: closed until 2017
ADDITIONAL CLOSING DATE > Sint-Jans-huis Mill: 5/5 (1.00 p.m.-5.00 p.m.)
PRICE > € 3.00; 65+ and youngsters aged 12 to 25: € 2.00; children under 12: free; Brugge City Card: free
INFO > Kruisvest, tel. +32 (0)50 44 87 43, www.museabrugge.be

♿ 23 Sint-Salvators-kathedraal (Saint Saviour's Cathedral)

Bruges' oldest parish church (12th-15th century) has amongst its treasures a rood loft with an organ, medieval tombs, Brussels tapestries and a rich collection of Flemish paintings (14th-18th century). The treasure-chamber displays, amongst others, paintings by Dieric Bouts, Hugo van der Goes and other Flemish primitives.
OPEN > Cathedral: Monday to Friday 10.00 a.m.-1.00 p.m. and 2.00 p.m.-5.30 p.m.; Saturday, 10.00 a.m.-1.00 p.m. and 2.00 p.m.-3.30 p.m.; Sunday, 11.30 a.m.-12.00 p.m. and 2.00 p.m.-5.00 p.m.; the cathedral is not open to the public during masses; Treasury: daily (except Saturday), 2.00 p.m.-

5.00 p.m. Useful to know: restoration work is currently being carried out in the cathedral. This can influence the opening hours of the treasure-chamber.
ADDITIONAL CLOSING DATES > Cathedral (afternoon) and treasury (all day): 1/1, 5/5, 24/12 and 25/12
PRICE > Cathedral and Treasury: free
INFO > Steenstraat, tel. +32 (0)50 33 61 88, www.sintsalvator.be

42 Schuttersgilde Sint-Sebastiaan (Saint Sebastian's Archers Guild)

The Guild of Saint Sebastian is an archers' guild that has already been in existence for more than 600 years, which is unprecedented anywhere in the world. The members of this longbow guild are exclusively male, with two notable exceptions: Queen Mathilde of Belgium and the Queen of England. A visit includes the royal chamber, the chapel chamber and the garden.
OPEN > During the period 28/3 to 30/9: Tuesday to Thursday, 10.00 a.m.-12.00 p.m. and Saturday, 2.00 p.m.-5.00 p.m.; during the period 1/10 to 27/3: Tuesday to Thursday and Saturday, 2.00 p.m.-5.00 p.m.

ADDITIONAL CLOSING DATES >
18/6 to 22/6
PRICE > € 3.00
INFO > Carmersstraat 174, tel. +32 (0)50
33 16 26, www.sebastiaansgilde.be

🏙 ♿ 09 43 Stadhuis (City Hall)

Bruges' City Hall (1376) is one of the oldest in the Low Countries. It is from here that the city has been governed for more than 600 years. An absolute masterpiece is the Gothic Hall, with its late 19th-century murals and polychrome vault. The adjoining historic hall calls up the city council's history with a number of authentic documents and works of art. A multimedia exhibition on the ground floor illustrates the evolution of the Burg Square.
OPEN > Daily, 9.30 a.m.-5.00 p.m.,
last admission: 4.30 p.m.

ADDITIONAL CLOSING DATES >
1/1, 5/5 (1.00 p.m.-5.00 p.m.) and 25/12
PRICE > Including Liberty of Bruges:
€ 4.00; 65+ and youngsters aged 12
to 25: € 3.00; children under 12: free;
Brugge City Card: free
INFO > Burg 12, tel. +32 (0)50 44 87 43,
www.museabrugge.be

🏙 45 Volkskundemuseum (Folklore Museum)

These renovated 17th century, single-room dwellings accommodate, amongst other things, a classroom, a millinery, a pharmacy, a confectionery shop, a grocery shop and an authentic bedroom interior. You can also admire a beautiful lace collection on the upper floor. Every first and third Thursday of the month (except for public holidays), those with a sweet tooth can attend a demonstration given by the 'spekken-bakker' (sweetmaker). You can relax in the museum inn, 'De Zwarte Kat' (The Black Cat) or in the garden, where you can try out traditional folk games on the terrace.
OPEN > Museum and Inn: Tuesday to Sunday, 9.30 a.m.-5.00 p.m., last ad-

mission: 4.30 p.m. (open on Easter Monday and Whit Monday)

ADDITIONAL CLOSING DATES > 1/1, 5/5 (1.00 p.m.-5.00 p.m.) and 25/12

PRICE > € 4.00; 65+ and youngsters aged 12 to 25: € 3.00; children under 12: free; Brugge City Card: free; a combination ticket is possible *(see below)*

INFO > Balstraat 43, tel. +32 (0)50 44 87 43, www.museabrugge.be

TAKE ADVANTAGE!

» Brugge City Card

With the Brugge City Card, you get free entrance 🎫 to 27 museums and other sites of interest in the centre of Bruges and a minimum 25% discount 🎫 at various attractions and museums outside Bruges. The Brugge City Card can be purchased from the ℹ️ tourist offices on Markt (Historium), 't Zand (Concertgebouw), and the Stationsplein (Station Square – Railway station). You can also purchase the discount card online via www.bruggecitycard.be.

For more information about the Brugge City Card, see page 12.

» Museum Pass

With the Museum Pass you can visit the different Musea Brugge locations as often as you like for just € 20.00 (www. museabrugge.be). Youngsters aged 12 to 25 pay just € 15.00. The pass is valid for three consecutive days and can be purchased at all Musea Brugge locations (except for the Liberty of Bruges) and at the ℹ️ tourist office 't Zand (Concertgebouw).

» Combination ticket Historium/Groeninge Museum

Experience the Golden Age of Bruges in the Historium, with the painting of *Madonna and Child with Canon Joris van der Paele* by Jan van Eyck as your leitmotif. Then see the masterpiece itself in the Groeninge Museum, along with the great works of many others of the so-called Flemish primitives. This € 17.50 combination ticket is only available in the Historium.

» Combination ticket Choco-Story/Diamond Museum

Combine a tasty visit to Choco-Story with a dazzling look at the Diamond Museum. This combination ticket costs € 17.00 (including diamond-cutting demonstration) or € 14.00 (without demonstration). For sale at the above-mentioned museums and at ℹ️ 't Zand (Concertgebouw).

» Combination ticket Choco-Story/Lumina Domestica/Belgian Fries Museum

Visit these three museums at reduced rates.

» Combination ticket Choco-Story/Belgian Fries Museum: € 13.00; 65+ and students: € 11.00; children aged 6 to 11: € 8.00; children under 6: free
» Combination ticket Choco-Story/Lumina Domestica: € 10.00; 65+ and students: € 9.00; children aged 6 to 11: € 7.00; children under 6: free
» Combination ticket (3 museums): € 15.00; 65+ and students: € 13.00; children aged 6 to 11: € 10.00; children under 6: free

These combination tickets are for sale at the above-mentioned museums and at ℹ️ 't Zand (Concertgebouw).

» Combination ticket Lace Centre/Folklore Museum

Combi-ticket: € 6.00, can only be purchased in either of these museums.

Culture and amusement

The city's high-quality cultural life flourishes as never before. Devotees of modern architecture stand in awe of the Concertgebouw (Concert hall) whilst enjoying an international top concert or an exhilarating dance performance. Romantic souls throng the elegant City Theatre for an unforgettable night. Jazz enthusiasts feel at home at Art Centre De Werf, whereas the MaZ is the place to be for young people.

🏙♿ **17** Concertgebouw (Concert Hall)

This international music and art centre is one of the *1001 buildings you must see before you die*. It is a place that offers the very best in contemporary dance and classical music. The impressive concert auditorium (1,289 seats) and intimate chamber music hall (322 seats) are famed for their excellent acoustics. In addition, various works of contemporary art are also on display in the Concert Hall. Brugge City Card: a 30% discount on the productions that are indicated on the free monthly event calendar.

INFO > 't Zand 34, tel. +32 (0)70 22 33 02 (ticket line: Monday to Friday, 4.30 p.m.-6.30 p.m.), www.concert gebouw.be

🏙♿ **44** Stadsschouwburg (City Theatre)

The Bruges City Theatre (1869) is one of the best-preserved theatres of its kind in Europe and was fully restored in 2001. The sober neo-Renaissance façade of this royal theatre conceals a palatial foyer and an equally magnificent auditorium. This outstanding infrastructure is used for performances of contemporary dance and theatre and for concerts of various kinds. Brugge City Card: a 30% discount on the productions that are indicated on the free monthly event calendar.

INFO > Vlamingstraat 29, tel. +32 (0)50 44 30 60 (Monday to Friday, 1.00 p.m.-6.00 p.m. and Saturday 10.00 a.m.-1.00 p.m., closed 1/7 to 15/8), www.ccbrugge.be

🏙♿ **34** Magdalenazaal (MaZ, Magdalena Concert Hall)

Its 'black-box' architecture means that the MaZ is the ideal location for youth events. The Bruges Cultural Centre and the Cactus Music Festival both organize pop and rock concerts here. Major artists from the world of music and more intimate club talents can all 'do their own thing' in the MaZ. Rising stars in the theatrical and dance arts also perform in this perfect setting. Children's and family events are regular features on the programme. Brugge City Card: a 30% discount on the productions that are indicated on the free monthly event calendar.

INFO > Magdalenastraat 27, Sint-Andries, tel. +32 (0)50 44 30 60 (Monday to Friday, 1.00 p.m.-6.00 p.m. and Saturday, 10.00 a.m.-1.00 p.m., closed 1/7 to 15/8), www.ccbrugge.be

🏙 **20** De Werf (Art Centre)

De Werf has an excellent reputation in the jazz milieu and is a favourite venue for many Belgian and foreign jazz musicians. From the beginning of October to the end of May, there is a free jam session in the foyer on every second Monday of the month. De Werf is also a great place to pick up a theatre production or some other exciting podium performance. In short, this is a setting where people create, produce, present and are inspired! Brugge City Card: a 25% discount on the productions that are indicated on the free monthly event calendar.

INFO > Werfstraat 108, tel. +32 (0)50 33 05 29, www.dewerf.be

What's on the programme in 2016?

The list below shows some of the most important events taking place in Bruges. The precise dates are notified in the free monthly event calendar, which you can pick up at any of the city's ℹ️ tourist offices on the Markt (Historium), 't Zand (Concertgebouw) and the Stationsplein (station). In the tourist offices, you will also find the free monthly cultural paper, Exit. And, of course, for a detailed events calendar you can always consult the website at www.visitbruges.be.

January

Bach Academie

Bach learned his music at his mother's knee, but in 1705 he set off on foot to Lübeck to become an apprentice of Buxtehude, whose flawless piano technique and *Abendmusiken* concerts were without a doubt an enormous source of inspiration to the young Bach. In the sixth Bruges Bach Academy, you will witness the interplay between these two generations of musicians.

INFO > www.concertgebouw.be
(You can read more about Bach and early music in the interview with Albert Edelman on pages 104-107.)

February

Brugs Bierfestival (Bruges Beer Festival)

For a whole weekend long, you can discover Belgian beers both old and new in the Beurshalle. The festival brings together more than 80 Belgian brewer-

BRUEGEL'S WITCHES

The origin of witch depictions in art is inextricably connected with the persecution of witches in medieval times. It is perhaps less well-known that the typical witch image was first developed by Dutch artists, with Pieter Bruegel playing a leading role. His portrayal of witches was widely copied in both the Southern and Northern Netherlands.

This exhibition not only displays a collection of extraordinary 'witch art', including engravings by Bruegel, but also gives an insight into the influence that local events, public fears and natural disasters can have on the treatment of scapegoats in society. At the same time, the exhibited works also say much about Dutch society during the period 1450-1700.

INFO > www.museabrugge.be

ies, which account for the production of more than 360 different beers.

INFO > www.brugsbierfestival.be

Wintervonken (Winter Sparks)

Winter Sparks brings warmth and conviviality to the Burg. The third edition of this winter festival once again guarantees scintillating street theatre, atmospheric concerts and heart-warming fire installations created by the 'Vuurmeesters' (Fire-masters).

INFO > www.bruggeplus.be

March

Reismarkt (Travel Market)

An alternative travel fair in the City Halls. Under the motto 'Travellers help travellers', enthusiastic globetrotters exchange a wide range of tips and information about almost every type of travel and every destination you can think of.

INFO > www.wegwijzer.be

April

Ronde van Vlaanderen (Tour of Flanders)

This historic and world-famous race for professional cyclists will take place for the 100th time in 2016. The starting point is on the Markt.

INFO > www.rondevanvlaanderen.be

More Music!

The Bruges Concert Hall and the Cactus Music Centre once again join forces to make More Music!, an exciting encounter between diverse and contrasting musical worlds. The result is an intriguing total concept that takes the visitor on an adventurous four-day voyage of musical discovery.

INFO > www.moremusicfestival.be

Mooov filmfestival

This 10-day film festival, screened in Cinema Lumière and Cinema Liberty, shows the best new films from Africa, Asia and South America. The programme covers both artistically innovative movies and films with a social conscience.

INFO > www.mooov.be

Meifoor (May Fair)

For three fun-filled weeks some 90 fairground attractions 'take over' 't Zand, the Beursplein, the Koning Albertpark and the Simon Stevinplein.

Mei

Meifoor (May Fair)

Three fun-filled weeks with fairground attractions in the centre of Bruges *(see above)*.

Airbag Festival

This international accordion festival is already into its 7th edition. As in previous years, the festival once again promises to be a musical mystery tour, in which unusual combinations and adventurous genres are welcomed, not shunned.

INFO > www.ccbrugge.be/airbag

A CENTURIES-OLD PROCESSION

Every year on Ascension Day, under the watchful eye of a huge public, the Holy Blood Procession passes through the streets of Bruges city centre. In the first two parts of the procession, members of the religious community, various brotherhoods and numerous costumed groups play out well-known scenes from the Bible: from Adam and Eve in the Garden of Eden to the Passion of Christ. Next comes the story of Thierry of Alsace, Count of Flanders, who was awarded a few drops of the blood of Jesus by the patriarch of Jerusalem during the Second Crusade in 1146. This priceless relic was brought back to Bruges in a crystal bottle in 1150, since when believers have been able to revere the Holy Blood in the basilica of the same name. The final part of the procession is dedicated to the public veneration of the Holy Blood. Preceded by the Noble Fraternity of the Holy Blood, two prelates carry the reliquary through the city.

Dwars door Brugge (Running through Bruges)

About 7,000 runners set off on a 15 km route through the city. This unique running event through the historic centre of Bruges is no longer just popular with local people, but now attracts competitors from all over the world. For the lesser gods, there is a 5 km course and a Kids Run is organized for children up to 12 years of age.
INFO > www.brugge.be

Budapest Festival

A three-day festival of music with concerts by the renowned Budapest Festival Orchestra, conducted by Iván Fischer. Each musical piece performed by Fischer and his orchestra gains a new dimension. Not surprisingly, the Budapest Festival Orchestra is regarded as one of the ten best orchestras in the world. A must for all music-lovers.
INFO > www.concertgebouw.be

June

Triatlon Bruges

This quarter triathlon (1 km swimming, 45 km cycling and 10 km running) through the city centre and the area around Bruges is being organised for the 13th time this year. The event is exceptional because the swimming part takes place in the city's picturesque canals ('reien') and the athletes pass numerous famous tourist spots, such as the Rozenhoedkaai, the Dijver, the Burg, the Market Square, etc.
INFO > www.triatlonbrugge.be

July

Zandfeesten (Zand Festival)

Flanders' largest antiques and second-hand market on 't Zand, the Beursplein and in the Koning Albertpark attracts bargain-hunters from far and wide.

Cactus Festival

This attractive open air festival in the Minnewater Park serves up a cocktail of rock, reggae, world music and dance. Notwithstanding its international fame, the three-day festival manages to pre-serve a cosy and familial atmosphere, with numerous fun activities for children.
INFO > www.cactusfestival.be

Navy Days

In 2016, Zeebrugge will host the 35th edition of the Navy Days. This will be an anniversary edition, since the Belgian Navy will be 70 years old. Under the expert eye of Belgian and international sailors, you can hop from one impressive ship to another. There are also numerous free exhibitions and demonstrations.
INFO > www.mil.be/navycomp

Moods!

For two whole weeks, there will be musical and other fireworks at unforgettable locations in Bruges city centre, such as the Belfry courtyard. In unique settings, you will be able to enjoy top national and international acts at one of the eight evening concerts. What's more, the concerts taking place on the Burg are free.
INFO > www.moodsbrugge.be

CARILLON CONCERTS

Throughout the year, you can enjoy free, live carillon concerts in Bruges on Wednesdays, Saturdays and Sundays from 11.00 a.m. to 12.00 p.m. From mid-June to mid-September, evening concerts also take place on Mondays and Wednesdays from 9.00 p.m. to 10.00 p.m. The inner courtyard of the Belfry is a good place to listen.
INFO > www.carillon-brugge.be

August

Zandfeesten (Zand Festival)

Antiques and second-hand market on 't Zand, the Beursplein and in the Koning Albertpark *(see above)*.

Moods!

Musical and other fireworks in the centre of Burges *(see above)*.

Brugse Kantdagen (Bruges Lace Days)

From mid-August, the Walplein and the buildings of the Halve Maan Brewery buzz with lace activities: information and exposition stands, lace sale and demonstrations. Free entry.
INFO > www.kantcentrum.eu
(You read more about lace and the Lace Centre on page 86 and in the interview with Kumiko Nakazaki, pages 120-123.)

Benenwerk (Leg-work) – Ballroom Brugeoise

Put your best leg forward for a festival that is guaranteed to bring out the dancer in you. Spread across various locations in Bruges city centre, you will be swept along by live bands and DJs for a dance marathon at no fewer than eleven different ball-rooms, offering the most divergent dance music.
INFO > www.benenwerk.be

MAfestival

Each year this highly respected festival of Ancient Music – MA stands for Musica Antiqua – continues to attract the world's top performers to Bruges and Bruges' Hinterland (Wood- and Wetland).
INFO > www.mafestival.be
(You can read more about early music in the interview with Albert Edelman on pages 104-107.)

Lichtfeest (Festival of Light)

During the Light Festival, Lissewege becomes more fairytale-like than ever: as soon as night falls, thousands of little candles are lit in the centre of the white village. Poetry, background music, intimate fire installations, street art and street theatre complete the romantic picture.
INFO > www.bruggeplus.be

September

Open Monumentendag (Open Monument Day)

During the second weekend of September, Flanders organises the 28th edition of Open Monument Day, when it opens the doors of its many monuments to the general public.
INFO > www.openmonumenten.be/brugge

Kookeet (Cook-eat)

With star chef Geert Van Hecke as its patron, the sixth edition of Kookeet (Cook-Eat) will be organised in a stylish tented village at the rear of the station. During this three-day culinary event, thirty of Bruges' gourmet chefs will serve various gastronomic dishes at fair prices.
INFO > www.kookeet.be

Zandfeesten (Zand Festival)

Antiques and second-hand market on 't Zand, the Beursplein and in the Koning Albertpark *(see above)*.

October

Brugge Urban Trail

The Bruges Urban Trail is a unique 10 km running event, taking in several of the city's beautiful parks and many of its important historic buildings. By running and jumping your way around the course, you will discover these tourist gems and magnificent monuments in a highly original manner!

INFO > www.sport.be/bruggeurbantrail

November

Razor Reel Flanders Film Festival

A six-day-long feast of fun for the enthusiasts of fantastic films: from fairy-like fantasies to frightening horror films, and from new releases to classics and genre cult films. In addition to film screenings, there are also workshops and exhibitions. The many guests will include celebrated national and international filmmakers.

INFO > www.rrfff.be

December

Christmas Market and ice-rink

For a whole month you can soak up the Christmas atmosphere on the Markt (Market Square) at the Simon Stevin-plein; on the Market Square you can even pull on your ice-skates and glide gracefully around the temporary rink in the shadow of the Belfry.

December Dance

A contemporary dance festival that allows prominent choreographers to do their own thing. The 2016 edition will highlight the United Kingdom. Britannia rules as you watch the very best of the contemporary British dance scene, including the only performance in Belgium of a new co-production between

Akram Khan and the Bruges Concert Hall, as well as contributions by Wayne McGregor, Hofesh Shechter, Michael Clark and many others.

INFO > www.decemberdance.be

Bruges Christmas Run

This unique running event (6 or 10 km) for charity celebrates its 6th edition in 2016. The course takes runners through the festively illuminated city centre and starts at 8.00 p.m. on the Market Square.

INFO > www.lopenvoorhetgoededoel.be

Take advantage!

With the Brugge City Card you can benefit from a discount on many events. You can find full details in the free events calendar issued by the City Bruges. *(For more information, see page 12.)*

Eiermarkt

Tips from
Bruges
experts

Cultural capital Bruges

Albert Edelman
fills the Concert hall

Each year, the Bruges Concert Hall continues to attract an increasingly bigger and more diverse audience, and this is partly the merit of Albert Edelman. As artistic coordinator for Early Music, he manages to lure the very best ensembles to Bruges; a matter, he says, of pleasing both the local people and the tourists musically.

IDENTIKIT

Name: Albert Edelman
Nationality: Dutch
Date of birth: 3 October 1978
Has lived in Bruges for 4 years. Albert is artistic coordinator for Early Music at the Concert Hall.

The Belgians and the Dutch may speak the same language, but that does not necessarily mean they always understand each other. Albert Edelman discovered this for himself four years ago, when he exchanged the Early Music Festival in Utrecht, the Netherlands, for a job as artistic coordinator for Early Music at the Bruges Concert Hall. 'During the first weeks, I really had difficulty understanding people. When my local baker spoke to me each morning, I just stood there with a smile. But that's all behind me now. Flemish people think a bit longer before saying something, and I like that. There is also more distance between people here than is customary in the Netherlands. The locals in Bruges need more time to get to know someone, which is not a bad thing, and I love that. Yes, I like it here a lot.'

In the meantime, Albert now feels fully at home in Bruges and each morning, just like his fellow citizens, he cycles cheerfully to his work. 'I live near the Sint-Anna Canal, so my 'commuting' is extremely picturesque. A beautiful panoramic picture, with the Bruges Belfry as one of the highlights: 83 metres tall and comprising 47 bells, 27 tons of bronze and more than 500 years of carillon history.'

Different styles, no compromises

Add to this a varied, challenging job and my joy is complete! There are relatively few concert halls that pay as much attention to 'my' kind of music as the Bruges Concert Hall. Right from the very beginning, it was clear that early and contemporary music would both have a place here. This results in a very diverse programme; we bring a multiplicity of different styles, but we always try to tell a story with what we offer. In my opinion, music played on old instruments truly belongs in a historical city like Bruges: it is like an echo of what once has been. What's more, the musical opportunities

'You can also see that a long cultural tradition already exists in Bruges. This leads to an exciting interaction.'

offered by the Concert Hall itself are outstanding; its acoustics are absolutely top-draw. We can present all different kinds of genres, from chamber music to a capella, without having to compromise. Everything sounds good in the Concert Hall. Technically, the sound quality is always perfect, which is very unusual. In short, this is the place where you can enjoy music and dance in the best possible circumstances.'

And Albert also does plenty of enjoying of his own: 'I know less about contemporary music and dance, which is why I am making grateful use of my stay in Bruges to discover the delights of these genres.'

Fortunately, a lot of other culture lovers share his views. 'We have a very good and loyal public. People who are curious, who want to hear new things and follow our tips. We work with reasonable ticket prices, so that we can reach a wider audience. In the foyer before a performance you will see distinguished gentlemen in suits rubbing shoulders with young people in jeans. Everyone feels welcome here, whether they are local people or tourists. People genuinely come for the music – and not to be seen – which really pleases me.'

'You can also see that a long cultural tradition already exists in Bruges. This

THE MUSICAL EVENT LIST OF ALBERT EDELMAN

1. 'The **Bruges MAfestival** is one of the world's most famous festivals for Early Music. For ten days, a surprising range of concerts is organised at different locations in the city and its immediate surroundings. In addition, there are also numerous readings, workshops and master classes.'
   (For more information about the MAfestival see page 100.) www.mafestival.be

2. 'The **Bach Academie**, in collaboration with Philippe Herreweghe, has become a firm favourite with Bach lovers all over the world. About 30% of the visitors come from abroad. Each year, the festival weekend attracts leading international musicians and ensembles, who specialize in the incomparable oeuvre of Johann Sebastian Bach.' *(For more information about the Bach Academy see page 96.)* www.concertgebouw.be

3. 'The **concerts of Anima Eterna Brugge**. This fantastic orchestra explores the classic, Romantic and early modern repertoire. They perform on historical instruments and with great respect for the original intentions of the composer.' www.animaeterna.be

BRUGES AND THE CARILLON: A SHARED HISTORY

The very first bells were developed in China, around 2000 B.C. The art of bell-making was then brought to the Roman Empire via Egypt and Greece, and from there arrived in Northern Europe around 400 A.D. Bells were soon used as a means to call the faithful to prayer and to warn the population of approaching danger. Charlemagne made the use of bells in a belfry obligatory at the end of the 8th century. Towards the end of the 13th century, bells were attached to mechanical mechanisms for the first time. In the 16th century, rich cities like Bruges added grandeur to their belfries and church towers by adding more and more bells. And so the carillon - the oldest (and biggest) musical mass medium in history - was born! In the 17th century, the technique was refined and from the 18th century onwards the carillon truly began to function as an independent musical instrument. Since the beginning of the 20th century, the art of carillon playing has undergone international expansion. In November 2014, UNESCO recognized Belgian carillon culture as an intangible item of world cultural heritage. The Bruges Belfry boasts a triumphal bell from 1680, which is two metres in diameter and weighs 6 tons. The bells in the current carillon largely date from the 18th century and were recently renovated. For more than 500 years, bell music has rung out across the city. On Monday and Wednesday evenings in summer, the free concerts attract lots of people to the inner courtyard of the Belfry. The carillon also plays every Wednesday, Saturday and Sunday from 11.00 a.m. to 12.00 p.m.

leads to an exciting interaction. We challenge the audience, and in return they let us know what they want to hear and see.' In order to keep that audience captivated, Albert regularly goes on reconnaissance trips. 'I have the opportunity to see and hear many new things, both here and abroad. In this way, I keep up to date with everything happening in the music world. By meeting other musicians, it is possible to make plans together, which

in turn often leads to unique custom-written programmes that are mainly performed in Bruges. In addition, I am constantly searching for young, fresh talent. Many young people are active in music from the Middle Ages, the Renaissance and the Baroque period, so there are plenty of new initiatives. In my mind, there is no doubt: Early Music is alive and kicking, more so than ever before! And certainly in Bruges!'

Albert Edelman
Best addresses

FAVOURITE SPOT

» **Sint-Janshospitaal (St. John's Hospital)**, Dijver 12, 8000 Brugge

'There are not too many works in the **St. John's Hospital**, so you can really concentrate on the Memlings. The impressive attic is ideal for performances and exhibitions.'

RESTAURANTS

» **Bistro Bruut**, Meestraat 9, tel +32 (0)50 69 55 09, www.bistrobruut.be, closed during the weekends and from Monday to Friday in the mornings (until 12.00 p.m.) and afternoons (2.30 p.m. to 7.00 p.m.).

'In a short space of time, this place has become a reference for every Bruges foodie. In here, you can enjoy a delicious meal in a simple setting with a relaxed atmosphere. Top gastronomy without frills.'

» **Bistro Refter**, Molenmeers 2, tel. +32 (0)50 44 49 00, www.bistrorefter.com, closed on Sunday and Monday

'People who cannot afford the magnificence of De Karmeliet can find a decent alternative here. What's more, this affordable bistro run by three-star chef Geert Van Hecke has a heavenly terrace.'

» **Bistro Christophe**, Garenmarkt 34, tel. +32 (0)50 34 48 92, www.christophe-
brugge.be, closed on Tuesday, Wednesday and during the day (until 6.00 p.m.)
'This evening and night bistro serves French classics and seasonal suggestions
until the early hours. Ideal for anyone who wants a nice dinner after a show.'

» **Trattoria Trium**, Academiestraat 23, tel. +32 (0)50 33 30 60,
www.trattoriatrium.be, closed on Monday
'My favourite Italian place in Bruges. Of course, there is a wide choice of pastas
and pizzas (you can even order an extra portion to take home!), accompanied by
fine Italian wines, cheeses or a little dessert.'

» **Bhavani**, Simon Stevinplein 5, tel. +32 (0)50 33 90 25, www.bhavani.be,
closed on Wednesday and Thursday
'A little piece of Bombay in the Simon Stevin Square. Here you can enjoy the
more refined Indian cooking, whether in summer on the terrace or in winter
around the cosy open fire. And Ganesh saw that it was good.'

CAFÉS

» **Craenenburg**, Markt 16, tel. +32 (0)50
33 34 02, www.craenenburg.be,
closed on Sunday
'The Craenenburg is rightly proud of its
unique terrace. It is also the best place
to hear the Belfry, Bruges' greatest and
most beautiful musical instrument, in
all its glory.'

» **Concertgebouwcafé**, 't Zand 34, tel. +32 (0)50 47 69 99, www.concertgebouw.
be/café, closed from July to mid-September (but open during the MAfestival); in
the period mid-September to June closed from Sunday to Tuesday (but open on
performance days, 1 hour before the performance starts)
'Of course, it is impossible for me to exclude the Concert Hall café from this little
list. It's the perfect place to hang out before and after shows. You can also pop in
during the day to order one of the suggestions or just have a coffee.'

» De Republiek, Sint-Jakobsstraat 36, tel. +32 (0)50 73 47 64, www.cafede republiek.be, no closing day, but closed every morning (until 11.00 a.m.)
'The Republiek recently rose, phoenix-like, from its ashes and now boasts a brand new interior. Fortunately, the huge walled inner courtyard remains unchanged. A pleasant spot to sit and chat, or simply to enjoy the sun.'

» Parazzar, Torhoutse Steenweg 10, tel. +32 (0)50 33 55 28, www.parazzar.be, closed on Sunday, public holidays and during the day (until 4.00 p.m., on Saturdays until 6.00 p.m.)
'Just outside the old city walls and perhaps less easy to get to, but well worth the detour. A cosy and traditional 'brown' pub that offers decent cocktails, seasonal suggestions and the better café snacks anno 2016. What's more, there are often performances here.'

» Groot Vlaenderen, Vlamingstraat 94, tel. +32 (0)50 68 43 56, www.groot vlaenderen.be, closed on Monday, Tuesday and during the day (until 5.00 p.m.)
'A cocktail bar with the air of a chic hotel lobby. A place that could just as easily be found in Hong Kong or New York. On top of that, the cocktails are perfect and the seats incredibly comfortable.'

SHOPPING LIST

» Raaklijn, Kuipersstraat 1, tel. +32 (0)50 33 67 20, www.boekhandel raaklijn.be, closed on Sunday
'Raaklijn is an oasis of peace, a place where every bookworm feels at home - only to leave again hours later!'

» Vero Caffè, Sint-Jansplein 9, tel. +32 (0)50 70 96 09, no closing day
'This is the best address for anyone who really likes coffee. Add a rich choice of teas and fresh, home-baked cakes and pastries, and my happiness is complete.'

» **Le Pain de Sébastien**, Smedenstraat 31, tel. +32 (0)50 34 47 44,
www.lepaindesebastien.be, closed on Sunday and public holidays

'There is bread and bread. Only the best ingredients are good enough for Sébastien Cailliau, and you can taste that in every bite. This explains why you always have to queue here every Saturday.'

» **Rombaux**, Mallebergplaats 13,
tel. +32 (0)50 33 25 75, www.rombaux.
be, closed on Sunday, public holidays
and Monday morning (until 2.00 p.m.)

'Music fans can indulge themselves here to their heart's content. Browse through scores, pick out CDs or admire the wonderful interior; all is possible in Rombaux.'

» **Butik**, Academiestraat 12, tel. +32 (0)468 17 74 66, www.welcometobutik.com,
closed on Sunday and Monday

'A smart selection from the better Danish fashion world is what Butik guarantees. Small but beautiful could be their motto. You never leave this place without buying something.'

SECRET TIP

» **Lissewege**

'I live in the Saint-Anne district, a lovely place, but Lissewege is also highly recommended. Each time the MAfestival takes place, you can find me there. Thanks to the beautiful acoustics in the church, it is a fantastic location for concerts. The beautiful old barn in **Ter Doest** is also well worth a visit.'

For more information about 'the white village' see pages 77-78, 87-88 and 150.

Flemish primitives in the spotlight

Till-Holger Borchert sees respect
as the key to succes

He was born in Hamburg, he lives in Brussels and he thoroughly enjoys
his work in Bruges as he finds himself surrounded by six centuries of
fine arts, and especially the magnificent masterpieces of the Flemish
primitives. In 2002, Till-Holger Borchert was one of the curators of
Bruges, Cultural Capital of Europe. Today he is chief curator of the
Groeninge Museum and the Arentshuis.

IDENTIKIT

Name: Till-Holger Borchert
Nationality: German
Date of birth: 4 January 1967
This chief curator of the Groeninge Museum lives
in Brussels but works in Bruges. He is the author of
countless publications on the Flemish primitives.

'Bruges is an exceptionally beautiful city,' says Till-Holger Borchert. 'What's more, it is also a wonderfully liveable place, partly because of the clever and careful way in which the city has been able to mix her medieval character with a modern ambiance. As early as the 13th century, the concentration of wealthy citizens enabled Bruges to become the commercial heart of North-western Europe. In the 15th century, the Burgundian authorities took successful structural measures, which resulted in an increase of the population and had a positive effect on the city's further development. Just as importantly, Bruges was spared the many ravages of the so-called Iconoclastic Fury, which caused so much damage in other cities. That spirit of respect and tolerance still pervades the city today. I must say it is a great joy to be here. The countless locals and visitors will surely fully agree with me.'

'Nearly every day I go and greet two masterpieces.'

Madonnas from around the Corner

'Nearly every day I go and greet two masterpieces: Jan van Eyck's *Madonna with Canon Joris van der Paele* at the Groeninge Museum and Hans Memling's *Madonna and Maarten van Nieuwenhove* at the Saint John's Hospital. I am not saying that I discover something new every time I look at them, but my curiosity and my pleasure remain as great as ever. And I still try and find out new things about them. They just continue to fascinate me! I sometimes wonder why people from all corners of the world have always found the Flemish primitives so absorbing. The answer perhaps lies in the fact that for the very

INTERESTING TOMBS

The central feature in the Jerusalem Chapel – located in the Saint-Anne district – is the ceremonial tomb of Anselm Adornes (1424-1483) and his wife, Margareta Vander Banck (d. 1462). Anselm – scion of a wealthy merchant family, confidant of the dukes of Burgundy and a counsellor of the

King of Scotland – had this chapel built in the likeness of the Church of the Holy Sepulchre in Jerusalem, with the intention that he should be buried here with his spouse. However, Anselm was killed and buried in Scotland. Only his heart was later added to the tomb in Bruges. The decorative tombstone depicts Anselm and Margareta 'en gisant': lying stretched out with their heads on a cushion and their hands folded in prayer. Anselm is dressed as a knight, with a lion at this feet, symbolizing courage and strength. Margareta is dressed as a noblewoman; at her feet rests a dog, symbolizing faithfulness.

'Whoever enters the museum shop of the Groeninge Museum will leave with some wonderful memories, that I can assure you. Perhaps you will take home your favourite art treasures in the shape of a handsomely illustrated book or a reproduction on a poster maybe, or

depicted on a few picture postcards. And why don't you surprise yourself with an original souvenir? I have caught not only some of my delighted fellow curators buying just such a present for themselves, but my wife as well!'

first time in art history we are confronted with recognisable people and familiar objects that correspond to today's reality. Even a Madonna seems to look like the woman from around the corner. The Flemish primitives laid the foundation of an artistic concept that in its realism is perfectly recognisable and therefore understandable to a modern-day observer.

The Flemish primitives discovered the individual. Quite a feat. Those Flemish painters were also dab hands at solving the problems. They explored space in an incredibly skilful and sophisticated way, for example by placing a mirror somewhere in the room. In Memling's diptych, a round mirror on the left-hand side behind the Madonna reflects the interior she is sitting in. In it, her own silhouette is painted just a whisker away from the silhouette of the patrician Maarten van Nieuwenhove, Memling's patron. Truly magnificent. Are these works of art still capable of moving me? Absolutely. For pure emotion a painter like Rogier van der Weyden touches me more deeply than Jan van Eyck. The works of van Eyck or Memling impress me more with their intellectual and conceptual qualities. Van der Weyden and van Eyck: it is worth visiting the treasure houses of Bruges, even if only for the pleasure of enjoying these two opposite ends of the artistic spectrum.'

Till-Holger Borchert
Best addresses

FAVOURITE SPOT

» **The churches of Bruges**

'The great churches of Bruges possess wonderful art collections, containing pieces that wouldn't disgrace any top-flight museum. Don't forget to look up at the tower of the Church of Our Lady. It is, with its 115.5 metres, the second tallest brick church-building in the world. When in Saint Saviour's, do go and marvel at the frescoes in the baptistery. And Saint-Jacob's Church is worth its while for the impressive **mausoleum of the de Gros family**, because this sculptural masterpiece reveals par excellence the self-confidence and power of the Burgundian elite.'

RESTAURANTS

» **Den Amand**, Sint-Amandsstraat 4, tel. +32 (0)50 34 01 22, www.denamand.be, closed on Wednesday and Sunday

'In Den Amand I once saw a German restaurant critic copy out the entire menu card. You can't get higher praise than that! A small and elegant bistro, where you will find both tourists and local people enjoying the excellent food.'

» **Rock Fort**, Langestraat 15, tel. +32 (0)50 33 41 13, www.rock-fort.be, closed on Saturday and Sunday

'Rock Fort serves original, contemporary dishes with a modern twist. Their cooking is so good that the place is packed all week long. Local people love it, and I also like to pop in from time to time. But be careful: it is closed during the weekends.'

» **'t Schrijverke**, Gruuthusestraat 4, tel. +32 (0)50 33 29 08,
www.tschrijverke.be, closed on Monday
'This homely restaurant is named after a poem by Guido Gezelle, which hangs in
a place of honour next to the door. But 't Schrijverke is above all rightly famed for
its delicious regional dishes and its "Karmeliet" beer on tap.'

» **Tanuki**, Oude Gentweg 1, tel. +32 (0)50 34 75 12, www.tanuki.be,
closed on Monday and Tuesday
'A true temple of food, where you immediately drop your voice to the level of a whis-
per, so that you don't disturb the silent enjoyment of the other diners. In the open
kitchen the chef does magical things with sushi and sashimi, and prepares his
seven course menus with true oriental serenity.'

» **Den Gouden Harynck**, Groeninge 25, tel. +32 (0)50 33 76 37, www.dengouden
harynck.be, closed on Saturday (until 7.00 p.m.), Sunday, Monday and most
public holidays
'Den Gouden Harynck is a household name in Bruges, known and loved by foodies of all kinds. It is also one of the most pleasant star-rated restaurants in the
city – as anyone who has ever been there will tell you.'

CAFÉS

» **Delaney's Irish Pub & Restaurant**,
Burg 8, tel. +32 (0)50 34 91 45,
www.delaneys.be, no closing day,
but closed every morning (until
12.00 p.m.) and also in the afternoon
from Monday to Friday (between
3.00 p.m. and 6.00 p.m.)

'It's always party time in this Irish pub, with its distinctive international atmosphere. Delaney's is the kind of place where you can rub shoulders with the whole
world at the bar.'

» **The Druid's Cellar**, Sint-Amandsstraat 11, tel. +32 (0)50 61 41 44, www.
thedruidscellar.eu, no closing day, but closed every morning (until 11.00 a.m.)
'I like to drop in at The Druid's Cellar every now and again, even if only to watch
Drew, my favourite barkeeper, in action. Or simply to relax and enjoy a glass from

their wide range of Scottish and Irish whiskies. They always taste just that little bit better in The Druids.'

» **Café Marcel**, Niklaas Desparsstraat 7-9, tel. +32 (0)50 33 55 02, www.hotelmarcel.be, no closing day

'You can find this café right in the heart of the city centre. Café Marcel is Bruges' re-fined version of a contemporary vintage café. In other words, a café from the days of yesteryear, but in a tight, new design setting. Think of dark wooden floorboards, sim-ple lamps, leather benches and original wood panelling. You can pop in here for a tasty breakfast or an aperitif with tapas. A welcome new discovery!'

» **Den Express**, Stationsplein, tel. +32 (0)50 38 88 85, www.horeca-station-brugge.be, no closing day

'The Den Express station bar is ideal for people like me, who travel a lot. Here I can enjoy a quiet coffee before setting off on my journey, safe from all the hustle and bustle going on outside.'

» **Hollandse Vismijn**, Vismarkt 4, tel. +32 (0)50 33 33 01, closed on Tuesday

'Whenever I fancy one of the popular Belgian beers, you will probably find me in the Hollandse Vismijn. This cheap and cheerful 'people's pub' is on the Fish Market. It is the type of café where everybody knows everybody and where you always get a warm welcome. Cheers!'

SHOPPING LIST

» **Antiquariaat Van de Wiele**, Sint-Salvatorskerkhof 7, tel. +32 (0)50 33 63 17, www.marcvandewiele.com, closed on Tuesday, Wednesday and Sunday

'For art and history I was fortunate enough to discover Marc Van de Wiele An-tiques. This is undoubtedly one of the best addresses in a city that is rich in an-tique shops. The place to find unique, illustrated books from days long gone by.'

» **Boekhandel De Reyghere**, Markt 12, tel. +32 (0)50 33 34 03, www.dereyghere.be, closed on Sunday

'For all my other reading material I rely on De Reyghere, located on the Market Square. Foreign visitors feel instantly at home in this book and newspaper store, primarily because of the large number of international titles it has on sale.'

» **Den Gouden Karpel**, Vismarkt 9-10-11, tel. +32 (0)50 33 33 89,
  www.dengoudenkarpel.be, closed on Sunday and Monday

'The fishing family Ameloot have been running Den Gouden Karpel with heart and soul for many years. It is not only an excellent fish shop with an equally excellent catering service, but it is also a really great fish bar. If you don't want the bother of making your own fish dish at home, in the bar you can sample oysters (European or Japanese), winkles, whelks, Zeebrugge fish soup, crab claws, half lobsters, fresh-salmon quiche, shrimp croquettes, etc. For a fish-lover like myself, it is hard to walk past Den Gouden Karpel without stopping to buy something.'

» **D's Deldycke Traiteurs**, Wollestraat 23, tel. +32 (0)50 33 43 35,
  www.deldycke.be, closed on Tuesday

'In the 15th century the Spaniard Pedro Tafur was already praising Bruges for its wide available selection of exotic fruits and rare spices. The Deldycke caterer is proud to continue this centuries-old tradition. Here, all your culinary wishes will be fulfilled.'

» **Parallax**, Zuidzandstraat 17, tel. +32 (0)50 33 23 02, www.parallax.be,
  closed on Sunday morning (in January, February, July and August:
  whole Sunday) and public holidays

'I always buy my socks at Parallax, but they are also experts at stylishly camou-flaging my beer belly! Highly recommended for other fashion victims and the ves-timentally challenged! Boss, Scabal, Zilton, Falke: you can find them all here.'

SECRET TIP

» **Museumshop**, Hof Arents, Dijver 16,
  www.museabrugge.be,
  closed on Monday
» **Jerusalem Chapel**, **Gezelle Museum**,
  Lace Centre, **Church of Our Lady of**
  the Pottery and **Folklore Museum**:
  see pages 75, 84, 86, 88 and 92-93

'Whenever I want to take a breather, I saunter down Saint Anne's, Bruges' most striking working-class neighbourhood. You can still sense the charm of an authen-tic community in the streets around the **Folklore Museum**. The area boasts many fascinating places, too. Off the cuff, if I may: Our Lady of the Pottery, the Lace Centre, the medieval Jerusalem Chapel and the Gezelle Museum.'

The art of bobbins and pins

Kumiko Nakazaki hopes
to gain immortality through lace

It is now over a quarter-century since Kumiko Nakazaki from Japan
set foot in Bruges for the very first time. In the meantime, she has
blossomed into a true lace expert who understands like no one else
how important lace is for Bruges.

IDENTIKIT

Name: Kumiko Nakazaki
Nationality: Japanese
Date of birth: 8 January 1956
Has lived in Bruges part-time since 1989.
Kumiko is affiliated to the Lace Centre
and publishes books about lace.

At university, Kumiko Nakazaki specialised in French literature, more specifically the 19ᵗʰ century symbolic poets. But she felt nothing for an academic career. That is why she decided to go on vacation for a year; to try and figure out what direction she wanted to take with her life. It was in the middle of this 'career crisis' that she by chance attended a Belgian exhibition about … lace.

'I learned that lace can grow very old, can survive a very long time, and decided that I wanted to do something that would live on for many years after my death.' Straight away, Kumiko booked a tour through Belgium, stopped for a day in Bruges and ended up at the Lace Centre, where she immediately made clear that she would love to learn more about lace-making. 'I returned to Japan with the idea of living in Bruges and immediately applied for a student visa.' At first, Kumiko found the change of continents very difficult. 'During the

first years, you focus on the differences, but after a while you start to notice similarities.' As a result, she extended her visa nine times! After almost a decade, she had mastered the intricacies of lace-making and designing. She had even published a number of books about

*'As long as skilled and passionate people want
to make lace and are prepared to continually learn,
Bruges will remain the world's undisputed lace capital.'*

lace. In other words, she had accomplished more than enough to leave Bruges, but she couldn't bring herself to do it. 'Bruges has become my second home, a part of my life. I now have many friends here. And so for years I have been shuttling back and forth between my Japanese home and Bruges. Sometimes I work in Japan, sometimes in Bruges. Both places give me everything I need: I can start working straight away in either of them, without losing any time. In fact, I do just the same things in Bruges as I do in Japan: drawing, drawing and more drawing. There is not much time left over to do anything else.'

LACE THROUGH THE CENTURIES

The history of lace in Belgium has its origins in the 16th century. It is generally assumed that bobbin lace was invented in Flanders, while needle lace probably originated in Venice. Whatever the truth of the matter, lace production became artistically, economically and socially important in Bruges in the years around 1550. The trade was protected and lace education was regulated. The religious orders (in particular, the nuns of Our Lady of Assumption and Our Lady of the Immaculate Conception) played a key role training poor girls to master the lace trade in special lace schools, where they also received a decent general education. In 1847, there were no fewer than 87 lace schools active in Bruges.

From 1850 onwards, lace-making evolved into a cottage industry. During the second half of the 19th century there were about 10,000 domestic lace-makers at work. This was exploitation on a massive scale; the lace merchants paid the women less than half of the average wage at the time. However, after the First World War the demand for hand-made lace fell dramatically and today lace-making is virtually non-existent as an economic activity. Fortunately, the people of Bruges managed to keep the old skills alive and have passed on this knowledge from generation to generation. Did you know that a simple method to learn lace-making was developed in the Bruges Lace College (founded in 1911) and that this method is now used all over the world? The lace techniques are taught by means of different colours: simple and the same in any language! Nowadays, various training courses are still organised in the Bruges Lace Centre, revealing the tricks of the lace trade to an increasing number of enthusiasts from every corner of the world.

And why not visit the permanent exhibition in the Lace Museum of the renovated Lace Centre, located at Balstraat 16. (For more information on the Lace Centre see page 86 and on www.kantcentrum.eu.)

Straddling the past and the future

'Whenever I shuttle between Belgium and Japan, I always ask myself over and over why I ever left in the first place. I love Bruges, because the city radiates enormous grandeur but is also easy to come to terms with. You can cross it by foot in less than an hour. Bruges is a city on a human scale – which is pure luxury for me. I also love New York and Tokyo, but only as a tourist. In those huge cities, everything is so much bigger and faster; they are also too modern for me. Bruges cherishes its past and its age-old lace tradition is an inextricably part of the city. Here, lace is not merely something you find in a museum or buy in a specialised shop; in Bruges, lace is part of daily life. Virtually every inhabitant of Bruges has lace somewhere in his house. I am convinced that there are still many lace treasures hidden in Bruges attics.'

In order to survive, the lace industry in Bruges must be more than just a fine tradition. 'You have to strike the right balance. We need to respect the authentic traditions and the old techniques, but this is not enough; we must also dare to innovate and to give a more important place to creativity. With an open mind, without imposing any restrictions on ourselves, we must move forward towards the lace of tomorrow. The contemporary lace industry is standing with one foot in the past and one foot in the future.'

This is not always an easy position to be in – but Kumiko has managed it for decades. The Japanese lace expert successfully unites the two worlds: 'During my early years in Belgium, lace-making was a huge secret. It was an art that belonged to the city and was not to be shared. I was the first 'foreigner', for whom the lace door was opened. Since then, many dozens of lace enthusiasts from all over the world have followed lace courses in Bruges. And as long as skilled and passionate people want to make lace and are prepared to continually learn, Bruges will remain the world's undisputed lace capital.'

Kumiko Nakazaki
Best addresses

FAVORITE SPOT

» **Prinselijk Begijnhof Ten Wijngaarde (Beguinage)**, tel. +32 (0)50 33 00 11, www.monasteria.org
'Obviously I am not the only one who loves the **Beguinage**, with its white-painted houses and sober garden. It is a serene oasis in the middle of the city, a place in which you can find peace and contentment.'

RESTAURANTS

» **'t Oud Handbogenhof**, Baliestraat 6, tel. +32 (0)50 33 71 18, www.hotel depauw.be, closed on Wednesday, Thursday and during the day (until 6.00 p.m., on Sunday until 12.00 p.m.)
'People have been eating at this site since the 15th century. And nothing much has changed. It is still the same atmospheric restaurant, where you can enjoy typical local cooking and seasonal dishes.'

» **Poules Moules**, Simon Stevinplein 9, tel. +32 (0)50 34 61 19, www.poules moules.be, closed on Monday (except in July and August)
'I only recently discovered this place: it is the address in Bruges for mussels, which is the specialty of the house. And if the weather permits, you can sit on the delightful terrace with its view of the Simon Stevinplein.'

» **Bistro Sint-Anna**, Sint-Annaplein 29, tel. +32 (0)50 34 78 00, www.sintanna.be, closed on Wednesday, Sunday and public holidays
'This cosy restaurant, where you can order home-made shrimp croquettes, steak or veal kidneys, is located in the shadow of the charming Saint Anna's Church.'

» **De Pepermolen**, Langestraat 16, tel. +32 (0)50 49 02 25, www.depepermolen.com, closed on Wednesday and Thursday
'In this restaurant in the always bubbling Langestraat you can enjoy one of their seasonal dishes or try their monthly discovery menu. King crab, carpaccio of beef, fresh soused herrings... Need I say more?'

» **De Middenstand**, 't Zand 20, tel. +32 (0)50 34 17 50, www.demiddenstand.com, closed on Tuesday and Wednesday
'It's great to sit on the terrace overlooking the square 't Zand and just watch the world go by. This address is famous for its fresh home-made dishes. The owner of the restaurant is also the chef – which is always a good sign!'

CAFÉS AND TEAROOMS

» **Li O Lait**, Dweersstraat 30, tel. +32 (0)50 70 85 70, www.liolait.be, closed on Sunday and Monday
'A good breakfast, a filter coffee made grandma's way, a *mocha latte*, an ice coffee, a glass of cava, a bagel or a piece of cake... At any time of the day, you can enjoy yourself at Li O Lait.'

» **Tearoom Carpe Diem**, Wijngaardstraat 8, tel. +32 (0)50 33 54 47, www.tearoom-carpediem.be, closed on Tuesday
'Located in a fabulous 17th century building near the Beguinage, you can enjoy the delights of the Detavernier Bakery and its attractive adjoining tearoom, where you can choose from their great selection of home-made cakes and other delicacies. It's a place where I enjoy coming to relax.'

» **Café Vlissinghe**, Blekersstraat 2, tel. +32 (0)50 34 37 37, www.cafevlissinghe.be, closed on Monday and Tuesday

'This is one of the oldest pubs of the city. The beer has been flowing here since 1515 and the original medieval bar really takes you back in time. During the winter, it's great to gather around the warmth of the stove; during the summer, you can enjoy yourself on the outdoor terrace near the petanque court.'

» **De IJsbeer**, Noordzandstraat 73, tel. +32 (0)50 33 35 34, www.ijsbeerbrugge.be, closed on Sunday (except in July and August, depending on the weather and the events)

'I only eat ice cream when I am in De IJsbeer, which has been making traditional Italian ice cream here since 1922. You can taste the freshness of the ingredients. Normally, I just stick to a cone with a couple of scoops of ice cream, but occasionally I treat myself to one of their delicious ice cream cups.'

» **De Torre**, Langestraat 8, tel. +32 (0)50 34 29 46, www.de-torre.com, closed on Wednesday and Thursday (except in July, August and during the (Belgian) school holidays)

'I like to drink a tea or coffee on the sunny terrace of De Torre, with its view of the Predikherenrei. And, having a sweet-tooth, I can almost never resist one of their delicious pancakes, waffles or a piece of apple pie.'

SHOPPING LIST

» **'t Apostelientje**, Balstraat 11, tel. +32 (0)50 33 78 60, www.apostelientje.be, closed on Sunday afternoons (from 1.00 p.m. onwards), Monday and Tuesday morning (until 1.00 p.m.)

'For almost three decades, 't Apostelientje has been the place-to-be in Bruges for hand-made lace of the finest quality, offering an excellent choice of both contemporary and antique pieces. The service is both knowledgeable and helpful. True professionals at work!'

» **The Lace Centre Shop**, Balstraat 16, tel. +32 (0)50 33 00 72, www.kantcentrum.eu, no closing day

'Lace-lovers must visit the renovated (in 2014) Lace Centre, which is located in the old lace school once run by the Sisters of the Immaculate Conception. You

can register to take part in a lace-making course and in the shop you can purchase beautiful pieces of lace and everything you need to make lace yourself.'
[See pages 86.]

» **Ark van Zarren**, Zuidzandstraat 19, tel. +32 (0)50 33 77 28, www.arkvanzarren.be, closed on Sunday (except in December, during the (Belgian) school holidays and from the beginning of the Easter holidays until late August)
'This is a great place to browse, right in the centre of town, where you can find different types of linen, fragrant soaps and special wallpapers. Romantic and rustic.'

» **Scharlaeken Handwerk**, Philipstockstraat 5, tel. +32 (0)50 33 34 55, www.scharlaeken.be, closed on Sunday, on public holidays and on Tuesday morning (until 1.45 p.m.)
'If you like lace-making or embroidering, you will find your way blindfolded to this handiwork Valhalla. Scharlaeken Handwerk is specialised in lace-making, embroidery and knitting kits. There is also a fine selection of books, special linen, accessories and exclusive lace material.'

» **Rococo**, Wollestraat 9, tel. +32 (0)50 34 04 72, www.rococobrugge.be, no closing day
'As long ago as 1833 Rococo was acquiring fame and fortune thanks to its unique lace creations. Nowadays, it specializes in the sale of traditional handcrafted lace work, both past and present. This is the address in Bruges for anyone who wants to buy antique lace. The shop also gives regular lace demonstrations and their expert staff will answer all your lace questions with great professionalism.'

SECRET TIP

» **Saint Saviour's Cathedral**, Steenstraat, tel. +32 (0)50 33 61 88, www.sintsalvator.be

'Now that the Saint Saviour's Cathedral has finally been freed from its renovation scaffolding, it shines like never before. On the beautifully laid-out cathedral square, you can share in the enjoyment of the children playing on the stone steps and the grassy lawns.' *[For more information about the cathedral see page 91.]*

Photogenic Bruges

Andy McSweeney shows us
the most beautiful spots in the city

His first visit to Bruges, now more than 15 years ago, made such an impression on Andy McSweeney, a Canadian with Irish roots, that he immediately fell in love with the beauty of the place - and decided to stay and marry a local girl. Nowadays, he guides photography enthusiasts who are still willing to learn around the city and shows them all the most photogenic spots.

IDENTIKIT

Name: Andy McSweeney
Nationality: Canadian
Date of birth: 8 December
Has lived in Bruges since 2000. Andy runs
Photo Tour Bruges. In this way, he combines
his love for Bruges with his love for photography.

It quickly became clear that Andy McSweeney, born in Montreal, was not destined to spend his whole life in Canada. At an early age, he drifted off to India, Australia and Europe, where, now more than a decade ago, he met his future wife in an Irish pub in Bruges. In almost every part of the world he has worked in catering, performed as a DJ ('I was the only one with good records') and... photographed the special places he encountered. During these wanderings he gradually trained himself to become a photographer, specializing in travel photography. 'Life as it is', perceived through a pair of keen eyes.

Andy quickly gave up on his catering and DJ career in order to focus fully on photography. And there is no better place to photograph time after time than Bruges. Nowadays, the Canadian organises photo tours through the city, in which he assists his clients with technical and artistic advice, while showing them all the most beautiful spots of Bruges. 'My strolls through the city are real workshops. Some of the participants are amateurs, trying to learn the basic tricks of the trade, whereas others are experi-

enced photographers, who want to discover the most photogenic places the city has to offer. And there are plenty of those to keep them happy!' What's more, Andy McSweeney is convinced that Bruges is one of the best cities in the world to explore by camera. 'Bruges is a safe city. You don't have to be afraid that someone is going to steal your expensive camera. And the city has such beauty to offer, both past and present, at every moment of the day and in every

The fact that Andy first saw the light of day on the other side of the ocean he regards as an advantage. 'Anyone who is born and raised here is used to all the splendour from an early age, so that they find it harder to take a fresh look at the city. I have seen many other parts of the world, as a result of which I can probably see more easily than they can what makes this city so special. I am convinced that I can see things that they can't.'

The photographer – not the camera – determines the result

season. While you are taking pictures, you look at the city with very different eyes and learn to focus on details that you might otherwise miss.'

When Andy is not busy taking groups around, you will regularly see him wandering through the city on his own, either

BRUGES ON THE BIG SCREEN

The fairytale-like and mysterious setting of Bruges has charmed numerous directors throughout the years. *The Nun's Story*, a movie from 1959 starring Audrey Hepburn, the prestigious British costume drama *The White Queen* (2013), the German romantic movie *Ein Herz aus Schokolade* (2010) and the Bollywood film *Peekay* (2014) were all shot in Bruges, as was the criminal comedy *In Bruges* (2008), which won several awards for its original script. Time and again the world heritage city has been chosen as the setting for film productions or tourist shoots. The most popular filming locations are the courtyard of the Belfry, the Market Square with its Provincial Court, the Wijngaardplein, the Jerusalem Chapel and the Gothic Chamber of the Town Hall.

In addition to the 'classics' (Rozenhoedkaai, Beguinage, Burg, Market Square, Minnewater and the canals), the tourist reports like to portray the lace-makers and chocolatiers of Bruges, as well as the windmills, the Church of Our Lady and the Holy Blood Basilica. Panoramic shots are taken from the roof of the Concert Hall or the Halve Maan Brewery.

ANDY'S 5 MOST ROMANTIC PHOTOGRAPHIC HOTSPOTS

1. **Groenerei** (City map: F8) – A typical view of old bridges and historic buildings, framed by just a hint of nature.

2. **Koningin Astridpark** (City map: G9) – This classic park is a hidden gem, with its small pond with fountain and the colourful kiosk.

3. **Jan van Eyckplein** (City map: F6) –This was once the commercial heart of the city. Nowadays, it is a very pleasant spot to pass a few hours.

4. **Langerei** (City map: G3, F4 and F5) – Discover the essence of Bruges at the Langerei, one of the most photogenic canals in the city.

5. **Bonifaciusbrug** (City map: E9) – The charming and picturesque Bonifacius Bridge, with the Hof Arents alongside, never fails to charm visitors with its sense of history and romance.

on foot or on his recumbent bicycle. 'A part of my job is to search for new and interesting views. Bruges has a lot of imposing monuments and landmarks, but the trick is to find the best way to photograph them. I always try to maintain a fresh view and pass this on to my 'students'. You have to leave the beaten paths, because it is here, away from the hustle and bustle, that you will find the real magic. On the Jan van Eyckplein, for example, you can be inspired by the Flemish primitives. In the tranquil Sint-Anna district we focus on classic lines. The important thing is that you don't plan too far ahead, but just let the moment happen.' And he has some other tips for future photographers: 'You don't need to own an expensive camera to take beautiful pictures. It is not the car that matters, it's the driver. And be critical: don't show your friends twenty different pictures, but just a single fantastic shot. Then they'll probably want to come to Bruges next year as well!'

(For more information about the Photo Tour Brugge see page 70)

*'Bruges has such beauty to offer, both past and present,
at every moment of the day and in every season.'*

Andy McSweeney
Best addresses

FAVOURITE SPOT

» **The Ramparts**

'I love **the Ramparts** surrounding the city and especially the stately windmills that remind us of past times. The turning sails exude a kind of peace and once you reach the top of the hill you are rewarded with a fantastic view over the city, all for free!'

RESTAURANTS

» **Parkrestaurant**, Minderbroeders-straat 1, tel. +32 (0)497 80 18 72, www.parkrestaurant.be, closed on Monday, Thursday and during the day (until 7.00 p.m.)

'The magnificent building houses the Park Restaurant is right on the edge of the Koningin Astridpark, one of the most romantic spots of Bruges. This restaurant offers Belgian cuisine with French influences.'

» **Bierbrasserie Cambrinus**, Philipstockstraat 19, tel. +32 (0)50 33 23 28, www.cambrinus.eu, no closing day

'This beer brasserie honours its traditional Belgian roots. Here you can choose from an extensive range of 400 different Belgian beers, served with local dishes based on Belgian beers.'

» **Bistro Pro Deo**, Langestraat 161, tel. +32 (0)50 33 73 55, www.bistroprodeo.be, closed on Saturday afternoon (until 6.00 p.m.), on Sunday and Monday

'A small workers house dating from 1562 now accommodates a cosy restaurant, frequented by both tourists and local people. In this bistro, you can enjoy traditional Belgian cuisine and fresh daily produce, made the way your grandmother used to make it.'

» **Restaurant 't Gulden Vlies**, Mallebergplaats 17, tel. +32 (0)50 33 47 09, www.tguldenvlies.be, closed on Sunday, Monday, Tuesday and during the day (until 7.00 p.m.)

'There are still some certainties in life. One of them is that the Gulden Vlies will open its doors at seven o'clock in the evening, from Wednesday to Saturday, and that you will be served food of the very highest quality. It's great for either a quick snack or a more intimate dinner. A really good evening-only restaurant.'

» **Pomperlut**, Minderbroedersstraat 26, tel. +32 (0)50 70 86 26, www.pomperlut. be, closed on Sunday and Monday

'If you want to step into another world, reserve a table at the magical Pomperlut. Small, but beautiful. Prepare yourself for gastronomic and visual indulgence on a grand scale!'

CAFÉS

» **(Eet)café 't Hof van Beroep**, Langestraat 125, tel. +32 (0)485 68 90 33, www.thofvanberoep.com, closed on Wednesday and during the day (until 4.00 p.m.)

'The Langestraat has many pubs, but the Hof van Beroep is the one that stands out. A class establishment where there is always plenty of atmosphere, with an interesting mix of locals and tourists. They have an excellent gin & tonic list and also serve great tapas and a delicious lasagne.'

» **Staminee De Garre**, De Garre 1, tel. +32 (0)50 34 10 29, www.degarre.be, no closing day, but closed every morning (until 12.00 p.m. or 11.00 a.m. on Saturday)
'This historic pub is hidden in the smallest street in Bruges and has a fine selection of delicious regional beers, as well as six draft beers, abbey beers, bottled beers and Trappist beers. Don't forget to try the tasty tapas.'

» **Joey's Café**, Zilversteeg 4, tel. +32 (0)50 34 12 64, closed on Sunday and every morning (until 11.30 a.m.)
'Local shoppers who have a sudden urge to hear a touch of the blues, jazz or rock, all hurry to this small 'brown' bar. It is located in the centre of the modern Zilverpand precinct, but is no less authentic for that. Concerts are regularly organised here.'

» **'t Brugs Beertje**, Kemelstraat 5, tel. +32 (0)50 33 96 16, www.brugsbeertje.be, closed on Tuesday, Wednesday and during the day (until 4.00 p.m.)
'The Brugs Beertje is a genuine classic, professionally managed by Daisy. This is the perfect address for anyone who wants to immerse themselves in Belgian beer culture. The beers can be accompanied by local farmhouse pâté or a Belgian cheese platter.'

» **L'Estaminet**, Park 5, tel. +32 (0)50 33 09 16, www.estaminet-brugge.be, no closing day, but closed every morning (until 12.00 p.m., on Monday and Thursday until 5.00 p.m.)
'A classic watering-hole for Bruges pub-hoppers. The interior is dressed up as an old-fashioned living room, where you can find excellent draft beer, good music and delicious bar food. In short, L'Estaminet has everything a good pub needs.'

SHOPPING LIST

» **LeeLoo**, Sint-Jakobsstraat 19, tel. +32 (0)50 34 04 55, www.leeloo.be, closed on Sunday
'LeeLoo is not only a trendy city boutique, but a cool shop with a soul inspired by the alternative fashion scenes of London, Barcelona and Berlin. Clearly one step ahead of the rest.'

» **Think Twice**, Sint-Jakobsstraat 21, tel. +32 (0)495 36 39 08, www.thinktwice-secondhand.be, closed on Sunday morning (until 1.00 p.m.)
'Vintage lovers and bargain hunters can browse for hours in this trendy second-hand shop that proves that nice outfits don't necessarily have to be expensive. Definitely a place to pop into on a regular basis.'

» **The Lodge Bruges**, Langestraat 50, tel. +32 (0)50 34 83 40, www.thelodgebruges.com, closed on Sunday morning (until 2.00 p.m.) and Monday
'In these hectic fashion times, The Lodge specialises in top quality men's cloth-ing. Everything you buy here is practical, timeless (the garments last for years) but also solidly reliable and respectable: the clothes are made with honesty and respect for professional standards. The Lodge is primarily designed to cater to men, but women and children will also find something to tempt them here.'

» **Depot d'O**, Riddersstraat 21, tel. +32 (0)495 23 65 95, www.depotdo.be, closed on Tuesday, Wednesday, Sunday and during the day (until 2.00 p.m.)
'In Depot d'O you can find great design classics, as well as African masks, zebra carpets, animal skulls and more unusual ornaments. It is a house of rarities, with a collection of objects that covers the entire world and an ever-changing display window. You have to be very quick, though.'

» **Kringwinkel 't Rad**, Langestraat 169/171, tel. +32 (0)50 34 94 00, www.dekringwinkeltrad.be, closed on Sunday and Monday
'This second-hand store is a fantastic place for anyone who likes rummaging around and hunting for bargains. Sometimes you can find real treasures here, sometimes your search will lead to nothing – but it will always be pure enjoyment.'

SECRET TIP

» **Bruges during the winter**

'For me, Bruges is at its most beautiful when it is covered in snow. In the win-ter, the city moves at a more relaxed pace, landscapes are transformed into frozen fairy tales and everywhere in the city you see smiling faces. In this way, Bruges becomes even more of a paradise for photographers!'

Focus on the Great War

Sharon Evans, in search of the First World War

Just a handful of kilometres from Bruges lies the Westhoek region. This green and pleasant land is now a haven of peace, but one hundred years ago, between 1914 and 1918, it was the setting for some of the most terrible fighting the world has ever seen. It was the Westhoek that first brought Sharon Evans to Belgium many years ago. Nowadays, this Bruges 'settler' leads visitors on tours of the old battlefields.

IDENTIKIT

Name: Sharon Evans
Nationality: Australian
Date of birth: 9 September 1965
Has lived in Bruges since 1991. Sharon runs
Quasimodo and organises bus trips to the Westhoek,
where she gives guided tours to many hundreds
of tourists.

Sharon was born in Asia, as the daughter of a serving Australian soldier. Having moved from place to place in that part of the world several times during her formative years, she eventually decided that the time had come to see what things were like on the other side of the planet! A year later, her wanderlust had still not been satisfied, and so she decided to 'hang around for a bit longer' in Europe.

The choice was between Bruges and Vienna. 'I felt that Bruges was smaller, prettier, cleaner and friendlier – and so I chose Flanders.' Today, many years later, this citizen of the world still lives and works in Bruges. Her very first visit to Belgium – and the reason why she was so determined to come to our little country – took Sharon to the Westhoek. This was the place where her great-

*'In the Westhoek I had the feeling that I was following
in my great-grandfather's footsteps.
Here in Flanders, I discovered a piece of my own history.'*

HIT THE ROAD WITH THE BRUGGE1418 APP

Using the special app 'brugge1418', you can go in search of the remaining traces of the Great War in the city. During your exploration, you will discover much more than just archives and museums. The app will take you to the Hof van Aurora (Aurora's Court), where thirteen spies and resistance fighters were executed, and to the Balsemboomstraat, which was the target of repeated bombing raids. It will also lead you to inns and taverns, where the soldiers looked for entertainment during the war years, to the house of the female spy Anna de Beir and to the city shop in the Cordoeaniersstraat. *(For more information see www.brugge1418.be)*

BRUGES, OCCUPIED CITY

Less well-known – because the history of the Great War mainly focuses on places at the front – is the fact that during the First World War Bruges was the German headquarters for operations on the Atlantic coast. Shortly after the German Marine Infantry had installed their occupation regime in the city, the German High Command decided to convert the harbour at Zeebrugge into a base for their submarine fleet. Bruges also served as a place of relaxation for the German Army and – for the officers, at least – as a place of culture. After serving at the front for a period of 3 to 6 months, German soldiers were allowed a stay of 2 to 4 weeks in Bruges, to rest and recuperate.

If you want to see and experience for yourself the places where the Great War was fought one hundred years ago, you need to travel to the Westhoek. You can find a number of suggestions in the chapter 'Excursions leaving from Bruges' (see pages 157-159).

grandfather, together with his many comrades, had fought side by side during the Great War. 'I am the daughter of a soldier, so I already knew quite a lot about the First World War. And I have always been interested in history; I guess it's just built into my genes! Besides, the Great War was very important for the Australian people. It's true that we lost

many of our finest sons, but out of that suffering we discovered our identity as a nation.'

The fascinating Westhoek

On her very first day in Belgium, Sharon immediately set off for the Westhoek. 'It's a wonderful place, with an undulating and easy-going landscape.' It was also an emotional place for Sharon. 'I had the feeling that I was following in my great-grandfather's footsteps. Walking where he had walked, remembering how he had struggled and fought here all those years ago... It was a really moving and deeply personal experience. Here in Flanders, I discovered a piece of my own history. People who have never been here before find it hard to imagine that this delightful countryside was once a terrible battlefield, full of misery and

THE RAID ON ZEEBRUGGE

During the First World War, Zeebrugge – the outport of Bruges – was transformed into a highly sophisticated submarine base, with the intention of cutting off the overseas supply lines to England. As a result, the British decided to attack the harbour. On

23 April 1918, Saint George's Day, a flotilla under Vice-Admiral Keyes made an attempt to block the entrance to the harbour, so that the German U-boats could cause no further damage. This famous raid, one of the most high-risk operations during the entire war, is still commemorated each year.

death. In Tyne Cot Cemetery, the largest British military cemetery on the European mainland, there is a huge memorial wall engraved with the names of 35,000 soldiers who went 'missing', whose bodies were never found. 35,000! Something like that cannot fail to touch you. In the meantime, I have been back to the Westhoek thousands of times, but I will never forget that very first time. And no matter how often I come, it never ceases to make an impression. It's that kind of

place; it gets under your skin…' In 1991 Sharon founded the forerunner of Quasimodo. Originally, she offered her tourist customers both cycling and bus tours, but she eventually decided to concentrate on the latter. Today she runs Quasimodo with her husband, Philippe. The couple have two tours: *WWI Flanders Fields Tour* and *Triple Treat: the best of Belgium in one day*.

(For more information see www. quasimodo.be and pages 156-158)

Sharon Evans
Best addresses

FAVOURITE SPOT

» **The canals around Bruges**
'As soon as you leave the city, you find yourself in another world: a green paradise. Whoever follows the Bruges-Ghent Canal or the **Damse Vaart** (Damme Canal), exploring the region by bike, is treated to one picture-postcard scene after another. Not to be missed!'

RESTAURANTS

» **Tête Pressée**, Koningin Astridlaan 100, tel. +32 (0)470 21 26 27, www.tetepressee.be, closed on Sunday and Monday. Only open at lunchtimes (11.30 a.m.-3.00 p.m.); on Thursday and Friday also open in the evening (6.30 p.m.-9.00 p.m.)

'You can find this foodie paradise just outside the city centre, but Tête Pressée is well worth the small detour. You will have a fantastic meal, you can watch the chef in action, and afterwards buy your own supply of delicious things from the adjacent food store. A varied address that it is a delight to visit.'

» **Taj Mahal**, Philipstockstraat 6, tel. +32 (0)487 14 74 86 and +32 (0)50 34 22 42, www.tajmahalrestaurant.be, closed on Monday and during the day (until 6.00 p.m.), on Saturday and Sunday (in the morning until 12.00 p.m. and in the afternoon between 3.00 p.m. and 6.00 p.m.)

'I was born in Asia, so of course I like piquant Asian food. I like to order my Indian curries from the Taj Mahal. Hot and spicy!'

» **Narai Thai**, Smedenstraat 43, tel. +32 (0)50 68 02 56,
www.naraithai.be, no closing day
'The Narai Thai is another culinary hot-spot: both literally and figuratively! Here
you can enjoy dishes ranging from the mildly spicy to punishingly peppery, and
all set in a trendy lounge atmosphere. It's almost like being transported to the
other side of the world, even if only for an hour or so.'

» **De Vlaamsche Pot**, Helmstraat 3-5, tel. +32 (0)50 34 00 86,
www.devlaamschepot.be, closed on Monday and Tuesday
'Eccentric, yet at the same time very traditionally Flemish. This sounds like a con-
tradiction but the Vlaamsche Pot somehow manages to blend these two extremes
together. In this somewhat unusual setting you can enjoy *waterzooi*, meat stew
(*karbonaden*) and mussels with chips.'

» **In 't Nieuw Museum**, Hooistraat 42, tel. +32 (0)50 33 12 80,
www.nieuw-museum.com, closed on Wednesday, Thursday and during the
day (until 6.00 p.m., except on Sunday afternoon)
'Carnivores will just love in 't Nieuw Museum, where delicious hunks of meat are
cooked over a charcoal grill. From spare ribs to best end of neck to prime steak.
And all in a delightfully relaxed atmosphere. Perfect for families.'

CAFÉS

» **Lokkedize**, Korte Vulderstraat 33,
tel. +32 (0)50 33 44 50, www.lokke
dize.be, closed on Monday, Tuesday
and during the day (until 6.00 p.m.)
'One of my very favourite places. A
pleasant bar where you can always enjoy some rhythm & blues, a bit of rock 'n

roll or a classic chanson. There are regular live performances and the kitchen
stays open really late.'

» **Bistro Zwart Huis**, Kuipersstraat 23, tel. +32 (0)50 69 11 40, www.bistrozwart
huis.be, closed on Monday and Tuesday and every morning (until 11.30 a.m.)
'This protected monument was built in 1642 and the facade and the medieval
bar-room are truly impressive. Since recently, you can enjoy a bite to eat, a
glass of something pleasant and occasional live music.'

» **'t Stokershuis**, Langestraat 7, tel. +32 (0)50 33 55 88, www.stokershuis.com,
closed on Tuesday and Wednesday and during the day (until 6.30 p.m.)
'Small is beautiful: that could easily be the motto of 't Stokershuis. A traditional city
bar in mini-format, with bags of atmosphere. A place you'll find really hard to leave!'

» **Bistro Du Phare**, Sasplein 2, tel. +32 (0)50 34 35 90, www.duphare.be,
no closing day, but closed every morning (until 11.30 a.m.)
'Bistro Du Phare is one of those increasingly rare addresses where you can
nearly always find live music. A place to be savoured: great on the outside terrace (overlooking the water) in the summer, and cosy inside during the winter.'

» **Café Rose Red**, Cordoeaniersstraat 16, tel. +32 (0)50 33 90 51, www.
caferosered.com, closed on Monday and every morning (until 11.00 a.m.)
'This slightly out-of-the-way café specialises in abbey beers and sells a good
selection of the world's very best 'trappist' brews, which you can either drink in
the pleasing interior or in the equally charming courtyard. And if you sample
one trappist too many, you can always spend the night at the hotel next door,
run by the same people!'

SHOPPING LIST

» **ShoeRecrafting**, Langestraat 13,
tel. +32 (0)50 33 81 01,
www.shoerecrafting.be, closed on
Sunday and Monday
'Luc Decuyper learnt the cobbler's art at
Delvaux and other famous names in the
leather trade, and is the man I can al-
ways rely on when my shoes start showing signs of wear. This excellent craftsman
obviously loves his work – and it really shows in the end result.'

» **Jofré**, Vlamingstraat 7, tel. +32 (0)50 33 39 60, www.jofre.eu, closed on Sunday
'Admittedly, this ladies clothing boutique is not the cheapest in town, but it has
an excellent selection of timeless designs that are well worth the investment.
The kind of shop that a woman could spend quite some time in!'

» **De Kaasbolle**, Smedenstraat 11, tel. +32 (0)50 33 71 54, www.dekaasbolle.be, closed on Wednesday and Sunday

'Whoever likes a delicious piece of beautifully matured cheese should definitely make their way to De Kaasbolle. From creamy Lucullus, the house cheese, through Tartarin Cognac (a fresh cow's milk cheese with Turkish raisins, marinated in French brandy) to the authentic Greek feta marinade: every one is a real treat for your taste buds.'

» **Da Vinci**, Geldmuntstraat 34, tel. +32 (0)50 33 36 50, www.davinci-brugge.be, open from 14/2 to 31/10, closed on Sunday morning (until 12.00 p.m.)

'Whether it is freezing cold or tropically warm, there are always tourists and lo-cal people patiently queuing up outside this deservedly well-known ice-cream parlour. The number of different flavours is almost limitless, and everything – from the ice-cream itself to the sauces – is made on the premises.'

» **Chocolatier Dumon**, Eiermarkt 6, Walstraat 6 and Simon Stevinplein 11, tel. +32 (0)50 22 16 22, www.chocolatierdumon.be, the shop on the Eiermarkt is closed on Tuesday; the other shops have no closing day

'I have been a big fan of Dumon's traditionally-made, top-quality chocolate for years. The Bruges story of confectioner Stephan Dumon began in 1996 on the Eiermarkt. In the meantime, he has also opened a sales point in the Walstraat and an impressive shop on the Simon Stevinplein. But I remain faithful to his small and welcoming shop on the Eiermarkt, where the old saying "good things come in small packages" really applies!'

SECRET TIP

» **City Theatre**, Vlamingstraat 29, tel. +32 (0)50 44 30 60, www.ccbrugge.be

'For me, taking in a concert at the City Theatre (Stadschouwburg) is a real treat. Bruges **Royal City Theatre**, in the very heart of the old city, dates from 1869 and is an architectural masterpiece. Every time I visit, I never fail to enjoy the waves of red and gold in the palatial auditorium and the opulent splendour of the majestic foyer. Little wonder that the Bruges theatre is regard-ed as one of the best preserved city theatres in all Europe.'

Lissewege

Discoveries outside of **Bruges**

The other Flemish historical cities

Antwerp (Antwerpen)   82 km

It is hard to describe Antwerp in a single word. This historic city has so much to offer: a beautiful cathedral and numerous imposing churches, a magnificent Central Station, the ground-breaking Museum on the River (MAS), the tranquil Rubens House, a delightful sculpture garden (Middelheim), a zoo with a history and so much more. Antwerp is also Belgium's fashion capital, home to many internationally renowned designers. That is why in the Scheldt city you will find dozens of exclusive boutiques, rubbing shoulders with fun bric-a-brac shops where you can browse for hours: it's every fashionista's dream! Not surprisingly, the local 'Antwerpenaars' – who are fairly loud by nature – are extremely proud of their city. Welcome to Antwerp, the most self-confident city in Belgium. **INFO >** www.visitantwerpen.be; there is a direct train connection between Bruges and Antwerp (journey time: 1 hour and 28 minutes; www.belgianrail.be).

Brussels (Brussel)   88 km

The whole world comes together in Brussels, with a different continent around every corner. It is a city bursting with life, from the exotic Matonge quarter to the stately elegance of the European institutions. The capital of Belgium has a vibrancy like no other and the formality of its 'hard' metropolitan structure is softened by the authentic, working-class ambiance of its more popular districts. On his platform not far from the majestic Market Square, *Manneke Pis* is permanently peeing. And this diverse city even knows how to reconcile the chic sophistication of the Zavel with the folksy informality of the Vossenplein. Royalty watchers rush eagerly to the Paleizenplein, art fans indulge themselves in the Magritte Museum, the Royal Museums or the Hor-

ta Museum, foodies hurry to the numerous food temples, and vintage-lovers climb to the top of the Atomium. And in the city where both Tintin and the Smurfs were born, comic lovers will have their every wish fulfilled, with more than 50 comic-strip walls and a renowned Comics Museum. In short, Brussels has something for everyone.

INFO > www.visitbrussels.be; there is a direct train connection between Bruges and Bruxelles-Central (Brussels-Central, journey time: 1 hour and 2 minutes; www.belgianrail.be).

Damme   6 km

To the north-east of Bruges lies the charming town of Damme. Until the silting up of the tidal inlet Zwin, Damme was the transhipment port of Bruges. To reach the literary home of Tijl Uilenspiegel (Owlglass), you drive straight along the banks of the Damse Vaart (Damme Canal), which is without doubt one of the most beautiful pieces of nature in all Belgium. The canal is lined with magnificent poplars, some of which are over 100 years old. Their wind-twisted trunks add to the charm of the setting. You can also experience their

beauty from the water. The nostalgic paddle steamer *Lamme Goedzak* travels leisurely and in style to and fro between the small medieval town and the Bruges' Noorweegse Kaai (Norwegian Quay). And every second Sunday of the month, Damme is transformed into a book centre, as booksellers from near and far come together to display their wares!

INFO > www.toerismedamme.be; scheduled bus no. 43 (not on Saturday, Sunday and public holidays, see www.delijn.be for the time schedule), bus stop: Damme Plaats; or by the paddle steamer Lamme Goedzak, www.boot damme-brugge.be *(for more information see pages 67-68)*. You can also easily cycle to Damme *(for bicycle rental points see pages 13-14)*.

Ghent (Gent)   39 km

No other people are as stubborn and as self-willed as the people of Ghent – or the Gentenaars, as they are known. It is built into their genes. In the Middle Ages, the Gentenaars revolted against Emperor Charles V and later they formed the first trade union, but they also built many great monuments and churches. You can admire the magnificent *Lamb of God* al-

tarpiece by the van Eyck brothers in Saint Bavo's Cathedral, before settling down on one of the many terraces along the Graslei or Korenlei. Afterwards, you can take in the stately Belfry, the much discussed new city hall and the less controversial old town hall (a splendid building with protected monument status). There is also the Gravensteen, a fortress built in 1180, and the nearby Patershol, a medieval neighbourhood full of crooked streets and winding alleyways. The House of Alijn, the Design Museum, the SMAK (Museum of Contemporary Art) and the STAM (City Museum) are all distinctive and thought-provoking. The same words could also be used to describe Ghent's large student population and the colourful vibe they create in the city's nightlife and cultural scene. The highlight of the year is the Gentse Feesten, Europe's largest city festival, which is organised annually in mid-July and sets the Artevelde city alight!

INFO > www.visitgent.be; there is a direct train connection between Bruges and Ghent (Sint-Pieters) (journey time: 23 minutes; www.belgianrail.be).

open to new ideas, which finds expression, amongst other things, in several remarkable architectural projects, such as the station, the 'Stuk' art centre, the Hoorn, the Depot, the Vaartkom district and the Museum M. All well worth a visit! And then there is Leuven, city of beer. With two breweries – Stella-Artois and Domus – located in the city centre and with several other traditional brewers nearby, there is no excuse not to relax for a few moments with a foaming pint. And what better place than on the Oude Markt (Old Market), possibly the world's longest bar...

INFO > www.visitleuven.be; there is a direct train connection between Bruges and Leuven (journey time: 1 hour and 28 minutes; www.belgianrail.be).

Louvain (Leuven) 110 km

Louvain is without a doubt the number one student city in Belgium. Dozens of historic university buildings are spread all over the old city centre. As a result, you come across students everywhere, moving from one campus to another. Leuven can proudly boast the largest and oldest university in Belgium, founded as long ago as 1425. Notwithstanding its age and tradition, Leuven is always

Malines (Mechelen) 90 km

Although the smallest of the Flemish art cities, Mechelen is well worth a visit. Situated halfway between Antwerp and Brussels, Mechelen is more compact than these major players, but still has its fair share of wonderful historic buildings and heritage sites. The River Dijle meanders through the city, enclosed by the Zoutwerf (Salt Quay) with its 16th century wooden frontages and the Haver-

werf (Oat Quay) with its pastel-coloured decorative facades. There is also the imposing Lamot brewery complex, which nowadays serves as a congress and heritage centre. Beautifully renovated in a daring and contemporary architectural style, it is a classic example of how upgrading industrial archaeology can bring new life to a city. But perhaps the most well-known sightseeing spot is the proud Saint Rombouts Cathedral; two carillons of bells hang in its 97 metre-high tower and are often played by students of the Mechelen carillon school. Another 'must' is the former palace of Margaret of Austria. The Netherlands used to be governed from here, but nowadays it is a great place for a quiet stroll in the inner garden.

INFO > www.visitmechelen.be; there is a train connection between Bruges and Mechelen, with a single change of trains in Ghent (Sint-Pieters), Bruxelles-Midi (Brussels-South) or Bruxelles-Nord (Brussels-North), depending on your day of travel (minimum duration: 1 hour and 20 minutes; www.belgianrail.be).

Ypres (Ieper) 46 km

Thanks to its flourishing cloth industry, Ypres, along with Bruges and Ghent, was one of the most powerful cities in Flanders in the 13th century. Its strategically important position in the Westhoek meant that the city was besieged on several occasions, resulting in the construction of strong defensive ramparts, which were further extended in the 17th century. Ypres also paid a heavy price during the First World War, when it was the scene of fierce fighting that left the city in ruins. It was rebuilt after the Armistice, and the most important buildings are exact copies of the medieval originals. The In Flanders Fields Museum now tells the story of the war through the lives of four of its participants, allowing visitors to experience the horror of the trenches and the bombardment of the city. Various (day) trips are organized from Bruges to Ypres and other sites of interest in the Westhoek *(see pages 157-159)*.

INFO > www.visitieper.be; there is a train connection between Bruges and Ypres, with a single change of trains in Kortrijk (minimum duration: 1 hour and 23 minutes; www.belgianrail.be); from Ypres station, it is approximately a 10-minute walk to the main market square.

The area around Bruges

BRUGES' WOOD- AND WETLAND

The Bruges' wood- and wetland is a green region surrounding the city. It is the ideal place to press the 'pause' button for a moment, allowing the stresses of daily life to gently fade away. Here, the clock ticks just a little more slowly and the good life is all that counts. Perhaps for this reason, the 'Ommeland' is home to several star-rated chefs, as well as numerous passionate regional producers. The pleasing canals, the open polders (that encourage cycling towards the coast) and the many historic buildings set amidst the greenery all add up to make a captivating region of great beauty and simplicity. The world heritage city of Bruges is the beating heart of the region, but the surrounding villages and small towns, steeped in old-world charm, are its soul. You can wander around in castles or soak up history in Damme and Lissewege. In fact, there is so much to do that you will be spoilt for choice!
INFO > www.brugseommeland.be

In the Bruges' wood- and wetland, your Brugge City Card *(see page 12)* entitles you to a reduction for visits to: the Uilenspiegelmuseum (Damme, 6 km, www.toerismedamme.be), the home of the legendary Tijl Uilenspiegel and Nele; the paddle steamer *Lamme Goedzak* (Damme, 6 km, www.bootdamme-brugge.be; *see pages 67-68*); Loppem Castle (Loppem, 6 km, www.kasteelvan loppem.be), where King Albert I took up residence following the liberation of the country at the end of WW I; the Mu.ZEE Permekemuseum (Jabbeke, 10 km, www.muzee.be), where you can stroll around the home, garden and workshops of the renowned painter Constant Permeke; the Roman Archaeological Museum (Romeins Archeologisch Museum - RAM) (Oudenburg, 16 km, www. ram-oudenburg.be), where you can marvel at the archaeological finds from Oudenburg's glorious past; Wijnen-

Wijnendale

Damse Vaart

TIP

An ideal way to explore the region around Bruges is by bike. You can design your own custom-made route using the brand new bicycle network maps (from March 2016 onwards). Alternatively, you can follow the signs for the Groene Gordel (Green Belt) cycle route.

dale castle (Torhout, 18 km, www.toerismetorhout.be), home to more than 1,000 years of history and a place of sad memories for King Leopold III; and the Torhout Pottery Museum (Torhout, 18 km, www.toerismetorhout.be), which focuses on the rich tradition of the world-famous Torhout earthenware.

COAST

The Coast never loses its appeal; it always has something for everyone. From De Panne to Knokke-Heist, each seaside resort has its own unique atmosphere. Old-world or contemporary, picturesque or chic, intimate or urbane, the seaside towns are all purveyors of the good life. Nature galore, an abundance of culture, wonderful sandy beaches, inviting shopping streets, traffic-free promenades that are ideal for a bracing seaside stroll: this is the Coast in a nutshell! And the regular tram service (www.dekusttram.be) allows you to travel from one resort to another in no time at all. Taste that salty sea air, enjoy the mild climate and treat yourself to a delicious meal with the very best the North Sea has to offer. You know it makes sense!
INFO > www.dekust.be

The Brugge City Card *(see page 12)* entitles you to a reduction for visits to: Seafront (Zeebrugge, 14 km, www.seafront.be, *see pages 89-90*), a maritime theme park where you will discover all secrets of the sea; the Port

Zeebrugge

Cruise (Zeebrugge, 14 km, www.
franlis.be; *see page 68*), where you will
explore one of Europe's busiest ports
on the passenger boat *Zephira*, taking
in one of the world's largest locks
along the way; the  Mu.ZEE Oostende
Museum of Fine Art (Ostend, 22 km,
www.muzee.be), with its unique collection of Belgian art from 1830 until the
present day; and the Mu.ZEE Ensor
House (Ostend, 22 km, www.muzee.
be), where you can enter into the fasci-

Zeebrugge, Seafront

nating world of Ostend's most famous
painter.

WESTHOEK

Endless panoramas, gently rolling hills,
open polders and breath-taking silence.
Once a battlefield of the Great War, now
a peaceful and truly authentic holiday
destination. In the Westhoek you will
discover tranquil villages, steeped in
history. An ideal place for great walks
and hours of cycling fun, with delightful
inns and charming restaurants at the
most idyllic spots, far away from the
hustle and bustle of daily life. Just sit
back and enjoy a stiff glass of *picon*, the
tasty aperitif so typical of this border region, sandwiched between the French
frontier and the North Sea coast. And

wherever you go, you are guaranteed to
get a warm Westhoek welcome. From
Bruges, various (day) trips are organised to the Westhoek *(see pages 157-159)*.
INFO > www.toerismewesthoek.be,
www.flandersfields.be

The Brugge City Card *(see page 12)*
entitles you to a reduction for visits to:
the In Flanders Fields Museum
(Ypres, 46 km, www.inflandersfields.
be), which tells the story of the First
World War in West Flanders in an impressive interactive manner.

Passendale, Tyne Cot Cemetery

Courtrai

From Lisbourg in France to the centre of Ghent, the Lys winds its way through a varied landscape. The flax industry created prosperity and transformed the Lys Valley into a dynamic centre of economic activity, focused on small and pleasant cities like Roulers (Roeselare), Waregem, Deinze and Courtrai (Kortrijk). The various museums in the eastern part of the Lys region and the new Texture museum, which opened its doors in Kortrijk in 2014, are also well worth a visit. The gently rolling landscape between the Lys and the Scheldt is ideal for exploring on foot, by bike or even by boat (there are several boat rental companies active locally). And whatever your mode of transport, why not take a relaxing break at the riverside and enjoy one of the typical red-brown beers that are only brewed in this part of the world.

INFO > www.toerisme-leiestreek.be

The Brugge City Card *(see page 12)* entitles you to a reduction for visits to: Texture (Courtrai, 44 km, www.texture kortrijk.be), a museum where you will learn everything about the Lys and its flax industry; Kortrijk 1302 (Courtrai, 44 km, www.kortrijk1302.be), where you will be catapulted back in time to the days of Flanders' most famous battle, which also has a Bruges connection.

MEETJESLAND: FLANDERS CREEK COUNTRY

Assenede

The Meetjesland is a region of ancient creeks and ponds, close to the Dutch border. During the First World War, the famous 'Dodendraad' (Wire of Death) ran across this region, but nowadays it is a haven of peace and quiet. Nowhere more so than in Sint-Laureins, where you can enjoy a delicious meal while taking in the spectacular views. More energetic visitors can explore the region around Eeklo by bike, making use of the extensive cycling networks and pausing to admire the forests, heather and peatlands in the Drongengoed landscape park. Really enthusiastic cyclists can press on to Het Leen nature reserve, or even follow the River Lieve as far as Ghent. Those who prefer a more relaxed form of travel can try the tourist steam train in Maldegem, before moving on for a little Second World War history at the Canada-Poland War Museum in Adegem.

INFO > www.toerismemeetjesland.be

The Brugge City Card *(see page 12)* entitles you to a reduction for visits to: the 🗂 Canada-Poland War Museum (Adegem, 19 km, www.canadamuseum.be), a double museum that reflects on daily life in Belgium during the Second World War and also tells the story of the region's Polish and Canadian liberators.

FLEMISH ARDENNES

The woodlands of the Flemish Ardennes conceal a surprisingly undulating landscape, ideal for exploring on foot or by bike. The tree-topped hills, the wonderful panoramas and the cobbled roads over which the cycling classics are raced annually offer an infinite variety of opportunities for tourists of all kinds. Admire the spectacular view from the summit of the Kluisberg, relax on the 'mountain' slopes in the Kluisbos recreational park or test the steepness of the notorious Koppenberg hill. Lovers of culture, heritage and gastronomy will be able to indulge themselves to the full in this

charming region between Audenarde (Oudenaarde), Zottegem, Geraardsbergen and Ronse.
INFO > www.toerismevlaamse ardennen.be

The Brugge City Card *(see also page 12)* entitles you to a reduction for visits to: the 🗂 RondeMuseum (RoM) (Audenarde, 49 km, www.rom.be), a unique visitor and experience centre that lays bare the soul and the heroism of Flanders' most famous cycle race (which starts in Bruges every year).

Audenarde, Markt

Audenarde,
RoM, RondeMuseum

Excursions leaving from Bruges

SURROUNDING AREA OF BRUGES BY BIKE

The Green Bike Tour

A guided trip to the polders, the flat countryside around Bruges. The tour pulls up at medieval Damme and other important sights along the way for a little extra commentary. Tandem rides can also be booked.

OPEN > Daily excursions, by appointment only. Reservation is required.
PRICE > € 18.00 (bike); € 36.00 (tandem); € 9.00 if you bring your own bike
MEETING POINT > Concertgebouw, 't Zand
LANGUAGES > English, Dutch, French, German
INFO AND RESERVATION > Tel. +32 (0)50 61 26 67, arlando@telenet.be

The Pink Bear Bike Tours

A mere five minutes away from bustling Bruges lies one of the prettiest rural areas in Europe. You ride to historic Damme, the handsome medieval market town, once Bruges' outport. Furthermore, a guide will show you the most enchanting places of the Polders. It goes without saying that there is also a stop at a pleasant café for some Belgian Beers and/or Belgian waffles. On your return

Damme

you follow the beautiful poplar planted banks of a canal and discover some of Bruges' best-kept secrets.

OPEN > Daily excursions, 10.25 a.m.-2.00 p.m. Reservation is required.
PRICE > € 27.00; youngsters aged 9 to 26: € 25.00; children under 9: free; € 18.00 if you bring your own bike
MEETING POINT > Belfry, on the Markt
LANGUAGES > English, but on request also Dutch or French
INFO AND RESERVATION > Tel. +32 (0)50 61 66 86, www.pinkbear.freeservers.com

QuasiMundo Biketours: The Hinterland of Bruges by bike

A tour through Bruges' wood- and wetlands, passing through medieval towns such as Damme, peaceful Flemish agrarian villages and dead straight

canals. A must-see for anyone who loves the peaceful greenery of the countryside.

OPEN > Excursions during the period 1/3 to 15/11: daily, 1.00 p.m.-5.00 p.m. Reservation is required.

PRICE > Including bike, guide, raincoat and refreshment in a local café: € 28.00; youngsters aged 9 to 26 and students: € 26.00. If you bring your own bike you pay € 16.00 as an adult or € 15.00 as a youngster (aged 9 to 26) or a student. Children under 9: free

MEETING POINT > At the town hall on the Burg, 10 minutes before departure

LANGUAGES > English, other languages on request

INFO AND RESERVATION > Tel. +32 (0)50 33 07 75 or +32 (0)478 28 15 21, www.quasimundo.eu.

(See also 'Exploring Bruges', page 72.)

SURROUNDING AREA OF BRUGES BY MINIBUS

Triple Treat Quasimodo tour: The best of Belgium in one day

Take it easy on this minibus tour, which takes you to, amongst others, the illustrious Tilleghem Castle and unique Neo-Gothic Loppem Castle. Included are a pleasant stroll through medieval Damme and a visit to the Gothic abbey barn of Ter Doest at Lissewege. And what would this tour be without some delicious waffles and mouth-watering chocolate? The tour ends with a visit to the Fort Lapin Brewery, just outside of Bruges.

OPEN > Excursions during the period 1/3 to 31/10: on Monday, Wednesday and Friday. Reservation is required.

PRICE > Including lunch and tickets to the Loppem Castle and the Fort Lapin Brewery: € 67.50; youngsters aged 8 to 25: € 57.50; there is an immediate € 10.00 reduction when you also book the Quasimodo WWI Flanders Fields Tour *(see pages 157-158)*.

MEETING POINT > You will be picked up wherever you are staying or at a pick-up spot in the centre of Bruges. Departure: 9.00 a.m. Return: 5.00 p.m.

LANGUAGE > English

INFO AND RESERVATION > Tel. 0800 975 25 or +32 (0)50 37 04 70, www.quasimodo.be

Loppem Castle

156

EXCURSIONS LEAVING FROM BRUGES

Vespatours

Discover Bruges' Hinterland in style: book a guided tour with a snazzy Vespa scooter and traverse the green polders, authentic villages and breath-taking landscapes. A couple of surprises are provided en route. Half-day and day tours. You can also opt for the Cook & Drive a Vespa arrangement, a daylong programme with a fun mix of cooking and sightseeing. If you prefer to explore the surrounding area of Bruges unaccompanied, you can also hire a Vespa *(see page 21)*.

OPEN > Excursions during the period 1/3 to 15/11: daily, 10.00 a.m.-6.00 p.m.

Reservation is required.

PRICE > Including helmet, experienced guide and insurance: half day tour: € 65.00 (1 person per Vespa) or € 80.00 (2 persons per Vespa); day tour: € 100.00 (1 person per Vespa) or € 115.00 (2 persons per Vespa)

MEETING POINT > Concertgebouw, 't Zand

LANGUAGES > English, Dutch, French

CONDITIONS > Minimum age of driver: 21 years, driving licence B, deposit of € 200.00 to be paid before departure

INFO AND RESERVATION > Tel. +32 (0)497 64 86 48, www.vespatours-brugge.be

TO THE BATTLEFIELDS

Quasimodo WWI Flanders Fields Tour

A guide from Quasimodo takes you on a personal and memorable minibus trip to Passendale, Hill 60, Messines Ridge, the private museum at Hooge Crater in Zillebeke, several Commonwealth and German cemeteries, trenches and bunkers, the Menin Gate and numerous Australian, New Zealand, Canadian, British and Irish monuments. In short, all the highlights! The stories told by the Quasimodo guides allow you to visualize the reality of four terrible years of war in the Ypres Sa-

Hooge Crater

Last Post

lient. It is also possible to stay on in Ypres after the tour has ended, so that you can attend the Last Post ceremony at 8 p.m. In this case, you will be brought back to Bruges by taxi after the ceremony.

OPEN > Excursions during the period 1/2 to 31/12: Tuesday to Sunday. Reservation is required.

PRICE > Including lunch and ticket Hooge Crater Museum: € 67.50; youngsters aged 8 to 25: € 57.50; there is an immediate € 10.00 reduction when you also book the Triple Treat Quasimodo tour: The best of Belgium in one day *(see page 156)*. People who opt to stay for the Last Post must pay the cost of the taxi ride separately.

MEETING POINT > You will be picked up wherever you are staying or at a pick-up spot in the centre of Bruges. Departure: 9.00 a.m. Return: 6.00 p.m.

LANGUAGE > English

INFO AND RESERVATION > Tel. 0800 975 25 or +32 (0)50 37 04 70, www.quasimodo.be. Tickets are also available from the ℹ tourist offices on 't Zand (Concertgebouw) and the the Markt (Historium)

In Flanders Fields tour

This bus tour will take you to numerous sites of interest related to the war of 1914-1918. With expert guides, you will visit the *Grieving Parents* by Käthe Kollwitz in Vladslo, the trenches along the River IJzer, the John McCrae site at Essex Farm Cemetery near Boezinge and the mine craters at Hill 60. The trip also

takes you to a number of remarkable war monuments: the Canadian *Brooding Soldier* (Sint-Juliaan), the French Guynemer monument (Poelkapelle) and the New Zealand Memorial in Passendale. The French military cemetery at Saint Charles de Potyze (just outside Ypres), the Belgian military cemetery at Houthulst and the world's largest Commonwealth military cemetery at Tyne Cot (near Passendale) are also included in the itinerary. The day is rounded off with a visit to the In Flanders Fields Museum in Ypres and the Last Post ceremony at the Menin Gate.

OPEN > Excursions during the period 4/4 to 25/10: Thursday and Sunday, and also on 8/11 and 11/11

Vladslo

PRICE > Including lunch and ticket to the In Flanders Fields Museum: € 75.00; 65+ and students aged 12 to 26: € 69.00; children aged 4 to 11: € 39.00

MEETING POINT > You are collected from your hotel at 9.45 a.m., departure from the bus stop at the Bargeplein/ Kanaal-eiland: 10.15 a.m. Return: 9.30 p.m.

LANGUAGES > English, German

INFO AND RESERVATION > Tel. +32 (0)2 513 77 44, www.brussels-city-tours.be, www.ticketsbrugge.be. Tickets are also available from the 🛈 tourist offices on 't Zand (Concertgebouw) and the Markt (Historium)

In Flanders Fields Museum

Flanders Fields Battlefield Daytours

Discover the most popular tourist attractions of the Westhoek and the Great War. You will visit the German cemetery at Langemark, Tyne Cot Cemetery in Passendale, the Memorial Museum Passchendaele 1917 in Zonnebeke, where you can enjoy a dugout-tunnel experience, the Menin Gate, the City of Ypres with its magnificent Cloth Hall and the not-to-be-missed In Flanders Fields Museum. The tour continues to Hill 60, Hill 62 (craters and bunkers), Heuvelland and Kemmelberg, Messines Ridge, the mine craters of 7 June 1917, trenches and various other war monuments.

OPEN > Excursions from Tuesday to Saturday

ADDITIONAL CLOSING DATES > No excursions during the period 10/1 to 1/2

PRICE > Including lunch, a local beer and tickets to the In Flanders Fields Museum and the Memorial Museum Passchendaele 1917: € 75.00; students aged 18 to 26: € 72.00; youngsters under 18: € 70.00

MEETING POINT > You are collected from your hotel. Departure: 8.30 a.m. Return: 5.30 p.m.

LANGUAGES > English, Dutch, French, German

ON REQUEST > Short evening trip to the Last Post ceremony at the Menin Gate in Ypres. Departure: 6.15 p.m. Return: 9.30 p.m. Price: € 45.00. It is also possible to combine the day tour with an evening trip or to draw up your own 'tailor-made' excursions.

INFO AND RESERVATION > Tel. +32 (0)800 99 133, www.visitbruges.org

Index of street names

Welcome to the World Heritage City of Bruges

LOOK FOR:
- Books
- Booklets
- CDs
- Charts
- DVDs
- Inserts
- Maps
- Music parts
- _____
- _____

There are places that somehow manage to get under your skin, even though you don't really know them all that well. Bruges is that kind of place. A warm and friendly place, a place made for people. A city whose history made it great, resulting in a well-deserved classification as a Unesco World Heritage site.

In this guide you will discover Bruges' different facets. There are five separate chapters.

In **chapter 1**, you will learn everything you need to know to prepare for your visit to Bruges. There is a list of the ten 'must-see' sights, a brief summary of the city's rich past, and a mass of practical information, including a clear explanation about how best to use the 'Brugge City Card'. This card will allow you to visit many of Bruges' most important sites of interest for free or at a significantly reduced price. This chapter also has plenty of useful eating-out suggestions for the lovers of fine food and drinks and shopaholics can discover the best and most authentic retail addresses in town.

The three inspiring walking routes included in **chapter 2** will take you to all the most beautiful spots in town. The detailed **map of the city** – which you can simply fold out of the back cover of this guide – will make sure that you don't lose your way. The map also shows the licensed places to stay in Bruges, offering a range of accommodation options that runs from charming guest rooms and holiday homes right through to star-rated hotels.

Chapter 3 tells you all about the different options for getting around Bruges and gives an overview of the city's vibrant cultural life, with a summary of annual events and a full list of the museums, attractions and sites of interest, including all its historic, cultural and religious buildings. Bruges' beautiful squares and enchanting canals are the regular backdrop for topclass cultural events. And few cities have such a rich and diverse variety of museums, which contain gems ranging from the Flemish primitives and beautiful lace work to the finest modern art of today. Put simply, Bruges is always an experience – whether your interest is art, chocolate, diamonds or chips!

In Bruges you can dine at a different star-rated restaurant each day or perhaps you would prefer lunch at a trendy bistro before wandering through the winding cobbled streets of the city? Or maybe you just want to take in a pleasant pub or one of the many magnificent terraces with a view? These are the places, full of charm and character, which you can read about in **chapter 4**. Five 'new arrivals' to the city will also tell you about their favourite places in town.

You are staying a bit longer in the region? **Chapter 5** suggests a number of excursions to the other Flemish historical cities, the Bruges Wetlands and Woodlands, the coast, the Westhoek, the Lys valley, the Meetjesland (Creek Country) and the Flemish Ardennes. The choice is yours!

Begijnhofbrug